Mountains and Passes:

Traversing the Landscape of Ethics and Student Affairs Administration

Patricia M. Lampkin
Elizabeth M. Gibson

Mountains and Passes: Traversing the Landscape of Ethics and Student Affairs Administration. Copyright 1999 by the National Association of Student Personnel Administrators, Inc. Printed and bound in the United States of America. All rights reserved. No part of this book may be reproduced in any form or by any electronic or mechanical means without written permission from the publisher. First edition.

NASPA does not discriminate on the basis of race, color, national origin, religion, sex, age, affectional or sexual orientation, or disability in any of its policies, programs, and services.

Library of Congress
12 270 628 02 1002 065 8

Mountains and Passes: Traversing the Landscape of Ethics and Student Affairs Administration. Patricia M. Lampkin and Elizabeth M. Gibson.
    p   cm. – (NASPA monograph series ; 23)
    Includes bibliographical references (p. xiii)
    ISBN C-93-1654-26-2
    1. Student affairs services — Administration — Moral and ethical
       aspects — United States. I. Gibson, Elizabeth M. II. Title. III.
       Series: NASPA monograph series; v. 22
    LB2342.9.L36   1999
    378.1'94—dc21   99-25139
                                                                                CIP

MONOGRAPH SERIES EDITORIAL BOARD

Patrick Love, *Editor*
Kent State University
Kent, Ohio

Marianne Bock, *Assistant to the Editor*
Kent State University
Kent, Ohio

Kristine E. Dillon
University of Southern
California
Los Angeles, California

Sandy Estanek
Alvernia College
Reading, Pennsylvania

Barbara Henley
University of Illinois-Chicago
Chicago, Illinois

Debora Liddell
University of Iowa
Iowa City, Iowa

Maureen A. McCarthy
Austin Peay University
Clarksville, Tennessee

Susan E. Mitchell
California State University
San Marcos, California

Robbie Nayman
Fullerton, California

Bettina Shuford
Bowling Green State
University

OTHER NASPA MONOGRAPH TITLES

Academic Integrity Matters

Advice from the Dean: A Personal Perspective on the Philosophy, Roles, and Approaches of a Dean at a Small Private, Liberal Arts College

Beginning Your Journey: A Guide for New Professionals in Student Affairs

Different Voices: Gender and Perspective in Student Affairs Administration

Life at the Edge of the Wave: Lessons from the Community College

A Student Affairs Guide to the ADA and Disability Issues

Student Learning as Student Affairs Work: Responding to Our Imperative

NASPA's monographs may be purchased by contacting NASPA at 1875 Connecticut Avenue, NW, Suite 418, Washington, D.C. 20009-5728; www.naspa.org; 202-265-7500 (tel) or 202-797-1157 (fax).

Contents

Acknowledgements vii

Introduction ix

Chapter 1:
Ethics and Student Affairs Administration 1

Chapter 2:
Do Your Part 17

Chapter 3:
A Principles-Based Approach to Ethics 49

Chapter 4:
Case-Based Approaches to Ethics 75

Chapter 5:
Virtues-Based Approaches to Ethics 97
with Leslie Rezac

Chapter 6:
Conclusion: An Ethic of Responsibility 123

Appendix A:
Suggested Readings in Ethics & Morality 135

Appendix B:
Guidelines for Ethical Analysis of Cases 143

Appendix C:
National Association of Student Personnel Administrators 147

Appendix D:
American College Personnel Association 153

Acknowledgments

The authors wish to acknowledge several individuals for their contributions to this manuscript: Miles Gibson and Aileen Walsh for their time, patience, editing, and technical expertise; Eileen Filliben, Melissa Wilbricht, Chris Fall, and Scott Petersen for their insights and suggestions; and Monica Nixon for her recommendations and attention to detail. Annette Gibbs, Carlos Gomez, and Wayne Cozart provided encouragement throughout the process. H. Samuel Miller gave continued technological assistance and overall insight.

We are most indebted to James Childress for his professional expertise, endless energy, patience, and guidance in bringing a rough idea to fruition.

Introduction

Deciding where to go is one of the most important decisions a hiker makes before setting out. The scenery and terrain of the mountains vary widely, so it is necessary to decide what kind of mountains best suit an individual's preferences, ability, and skill level. Some people prefer steep ascents, with craggy inclines and the opportunity to rock climb. Others favor gentler terrain, with lush vegetation and no need for gear. Knowing the kinds of mountains available and choosing which to pursue are the first steps in setting off for a day trip. As we explore the terrain of ethics and its relation to student affairs, it is important to recognize the three major mountains on the landscape. Principles-based, case-based, and virtues-based approaches to ethics represent three major approaches to the moral life. Some professionals prefer the methods advocated in one of these approaches, while others like aspects of all three. After all, when looking at a mountain range, it is not always easy to tell where one mountain ends and its neighbor begins. The passes not only link mountains to each other but also are themselves separate areas for hiking. We hope to find these passes and show the intricate relationships among these three major approaches to ethics.

Once a hiker has decided where to go for the day, she needs a map of the mountain. These abstract representations of the terrain will give the hiker some clues about areas that are potentially dangerous and about the different routes to the summit. Having this guide in her backpack provides a measure of security in case she gets lost, but it cannot tell her what it actually is like to hike any particular mountain. So, outfitted with her pack, map, and lunch, the hiker begins to climb. After getting oriented to the proper trail, she now must pay close attention to the terrain, which is not represented in detail on the map. Some mountains have well-worn trails and little attention is required when walking; others have rough markers indicating the path, but rocks and roots litter the way.

More than a map is thus needed for a successful hike. This book too can be used as a map for exploring the three approaches to ethics, but it cannot fully indicate what it is like to act within a particular system. Our map can offer some guidance when you are deciding where to go or are lost, but it cannot yield more specific details. In order to facilitate your experience in using these approaches, we present more concrete information through an actual case. Your background, personality, values, and interests will come into play in your use of this book as a guide through the landscape. Try to decide which mountains you prefer, and see if you can locate the passes between them. If none of the options we present interest you, Appendix A suggests other maps for areas of the ethical landscape.

Hiking can be very exciting at times, yet there are many routine steps along the way. We can develop a more comprehensive view of ethics by noticing the relationship between the long stretches of trail through a dense forest and the gorgeous view at an overlook. While we will offer some guidance for the exciting ethical crises, we encourage you to notice how ethics permeates every human interaction in your personal and professional lives. The forest has many riches that we tend to rush past in our quest for the summit, but in reality we spend the majority of our lives moving through more ordinary ethical landscapes.

OUTLINE OF CHAPTERS

Chapter One: Ethics and Student Affairs Administration

In the last two decades, several scholars in student affairs administration have published reflections on the role of ethics in student affairs. Karen Kitchener (1985), Harry Canon and Robert Brown (1985), M. Lee Upcraft and Thomas Poole (1991), and, most recently, Jane Fried (1997) have worked through complicated student affairs issues within various ethics frameworks. Despite their contributions to the study of ethics in student affairs administration, the articles of these authors presume a degree of knowledge about ethical theory that many readers do not possess. In this text, we provide a primer for ethics in student affairs administration and hope that it can serve as a foundation for further reading in ethics. The background information we provide should offer readers a framework for analyzing articles about ethics in student affairs. Recognizing the diversity of views on the ways to conduct ethical reflection and decision-making, we do not prescribe a single approach to ethics. Yet, we believe that mastering the major approaches to ethics can illuminate the process of moral reasoning, make us aware of our own biases, and help us appreciate the perspectives of others (Nash, 1996). We present and discuss several major approaches to ethics with the hope that this text will act as a catalyst for your own reflections on the role of ethics in everyday life.

The chapters refer to an extended case encapsulating the events of a real situation, present brief overviews of three different ethical approaches, with some assessment of their strengths and weaknesses, and elucidate the relevance of each approach to the case. These approaches reflect ethical orientations based on agents, actions, and circumstances, and the criticisms of all three approaches include feminist insights. Appendix A offers a list of suggested readings related to ethics in student affairs. Appendix B includes several different approaches for resolving ethical conflicts when the resources of preventive ethics are not adequate. Finally, Appendices C and D outline the professional ethics statements endorsed by the National Association of Student Personnel Administrators [NASPA] and the American College Personnel Association [ACPA].

Chapter Two: "Do Your Part"
Since our approach to ethics involves paying close attention to small details, Chapter Two presents a single case in great depth. Ethical decision-making in student affairs depends on the complexities of actual situations and the different ways that agents respond to these situations; therefore, we will present various ethics theories in the context of the case, a departure from previous approaches to ethics in student affairs administration. Rather than examining the ethics of residence hall conflicts, disability issues, or other specific topics, we will work through one complicated case and illustrate how different ethical theories would approach the various issues that emerge. The presentation of this case is quite extensive because one or two paragraphs summarizing the relevant facts of a case would merely constitute what *we* think is important. The very process of describing a case involves the writer's interpretation as she decides what to include and exclude (Chambers, 1994). Indeed, we have done "much of the ethical work already" when we describe a particular case, since a description inevitably reflects a moral judgment (Elliott, 1992, p. 28). A longer case presentation is not free from this filter, but by providing as much information as possible the complexity of the situation speaks for itself. Although we make no claims that the presentation of the case is neutral, we have interviewed several of the participants in the actual situation and asked them to contribute to the writing of the case.

The case, "Do Your Part," combines problems and everyday ethics. Since student affairs professionals face challenges in both areas on a regular basis, we hope this case will bring out the messiness of everyday ethics, even when the problem at hand is being resolved. Different ethical theories may yield very different approaches to the case because professionals of various moral orientations will focus on different aspects. Using the process outlined below when evaluating the case may help you decide which theory best fits your professional and personal values. Keeping these questions in mind can anchor reflections about the case and the role of ethics in it. Respond to the questions about your moral life before reading the rest of the book; revisit your answers as you read about the various approaches to ethics.

Process of Moral Evaluation

- **Make a list of your moral values.**

Here are some questions to guide this process: What moral values are important to you? (being honest, doing unto others as you would have them do unto you, maximizing the greatest good for the greatest number of people, honoring your ancestors, etc.) Do these reflect your cultural upbringing? Do you feel that you try to be a good person? How do you define "good?" Do you think that our responsibility is to leave people alone and let them make their own choices as long as they do not interfere with others? Or, do people have an obligation to try actively to improve their communities and others' situations? Do you try to treat all people with similar respect or do you give some preferential treatment? Is this preferential treatment justified? Are any of these values informed by religious systems?

- **Is there a difference between the way you conduct yourself professionally and personally?**

If the answer is yes, consider whether this difference is necessary or something that you have accepted from the community. For example, at home you may be very nurturing and value your relationships but at work may find that you are more interested in rules and justice. Is this necessary in order to maintain a sense of professionalism at work? Are personal relationships at work sometimes sacrificed in order to preserve communal stability?

■ **What do you think about rules in general?** (Chapter Three)
Do you tend to live your life in a way that follows principles, or do you often find ways to bend rules and look for exceptions? When you do break rules, how seriously do you take this? Do you feel guilty for a long time and try to avoid breaking the rule again or are you able to move on relatively quickly? For example, if you violate the confidence of a student when talking with a co-worker, do you see this as part of your job (seeking advice or support from other people) or as breaking an implicit promise? When working with others on an issue, do you first try to identify principles or policies that apply or are you more interested in the particularities of the situation?

■ **What role do circumstances and consequences play in your moral decisions?** (Chapter Four)
When trying to make a decision about how to act, do you spend a lot of time thinking through the circumstances of the situation? Do you think that particular situations allow you to justify behavior in which you may not otherwise engage? For example, would you lie to save a student from expulsion if you thought the judiciary system was being unfair? Do you focus on evaluating the potential consequences of your actions? If you thought that performing a specific act would create undesirable consequences, would this be enough to dissuade you from acting? For example, if you could extricate yourself from a sticky situation with a colleague by lying, would you do so? How would you justify this behavior if you were caught in the lie? Does it make a difference if the consequences affect you alone or if they also affect the lives of others?

■ **How do virtues, principles, and your community interact in your life?** (Chapter Five)
What characteristics are most important to you? How would you describe the most important components of a friendship or a working relationship? What virtues do you absorb from your community that you may not acknowledge explicitly? Is working long hours considered the virtue of a strong work ethic,

or does your community value professionals who lead balanced lives? In your personal moral life, if you think that courage is a virtue, would you break a rule in order to perform a courageous act? If a friend confided to you that she broke a university policy that didn't hurt anyone else, would you lie to the university police in order to protect her? Would you do this for anyone or just for some people? How do you draw the distinction?

■ **How do principles and relationships connect in your life?**
If you have to balance breaking a rule with nurturing a relationship, which is more important to you? Do you value a sense of fairness and justice? How does this operate in your relationships? For example, if two underage students were caught drinking in their residence hall rooms would you sanction them equally, or would you want to know more about their situations? Does each relationship warrant special consideration that cannot be compared to others? In a less personal context, would you advocate changing a policy that was damaging your relationship with students? What responsibilities do we have to ourselves, our colleagues, students, and institutions?

This process of moral evaluation is designed to help student affairs professionals identify the role that ethics plays in our lives. By recognizing the undercurrent of ethics in all that we do, we gain a new understanding of our encounters with others and have a different language with which to describe problems when they arise. Many of us have experienced the frustration of working with someone who has different opinions about how a policy should be implemented. Ethics can provide some guidance for discussing these "rubs" before they turn into full-blown conflicts. Yet, sometimes we do lose our way and face crises, in which case a map guiding us back to the trail can be helpful. In Appendix B, we offer several methods for resolving conflicts and making decisions in difficult cases. Since this conflict-oriented approach to ethics has received a great deal of attention in the student affairs literature, we focus on a broader role for ethics in the lives of student affairs professionals. For more detailed descriptions of this perspective, see works by Kitchener (1984, 1985), Canon and Brown (1985), Nash (1997), and Upcraft and Poole (1991).

Chapter Three: Principles-Based Approaches to Ethics

What principles or rules should guide one's behavior? In this chapter, we present a summary of major principles-based approaches to ethics. We highlight the work that Tom Beauchamp and James Childress presented in *Principles of Biomedical Ethics* (1994), since it provides a widely used principles-based approach to practical ethics. Although emphases may vary, principles-based approaches to ethics generally hold that commonly held principles and rules are the main source of moral authority. Thus, when faced with troubling situations, moral norms are our guiding force. Principles can be interpreted as having varying degrees of "bindingness" or authority in our lives. Some principles-based theories hold that the principles must be obeyed absolutely, whereas Beauchamp and Childress present *prima facie* principles. Principles deemed *prima facie*, which literally means "on first impression," are binding on moral agents unless a significant reason exists for overriding them. For example, student affairs administrators should not break the confidentiality of their colleagues or students; however, if a student reveals that he is suicidal, the administrator will have to decide if the threat is serious enough to warrant breaking the rule of confidentiality. An important aspect of *prima facie* principles or rules is that they do not disappear once they are broken; breaking a *prima facie* principle should lead to a sense of guilt or remorse.

The major strength of this approach to ethics is that it can provide a number of memorable principles or rules that can be used to guide behavior in specific cases. Principles are easier to teach than virtues or caring. It is also relatively easy to assess compliance with principles-based approaches to ethics: determining when someone has broken confidentiality may be less complicated than deciding that someone is not caring. Thus, ease of transmission and consistency are two major strengths of a principles-based approach to ethics. Gilligan (1993) and others, however, have demonstrated that many people, particularly women, do not think in this rationalistic, analytic way. This different mode of moral reasoning has important ramifications for student affairs as outlined by Gilligan (1981), Chickering and Reisser (1993), and Pascarella and Terenzini (1981).

This approach has its critics, however; some bioethics scholars (Clouser & Gert, 1990, p. 219) refer to the "mantra" of principles (autonomy, non-maleficence, beneficence, and justice) that inexperienced students chant without any real sense of the way they function in particular cases. They argue that principles are too *general* to be of any help and lack sufficient theoretical support; further, they claim that such generality leaves a great deal of room for abuse. Conversely, others have charged that principles can be too *specific* and thus only narrowly applicable. The use of rules in our moral life is unavoidable, and these divergent criticisms demonstrate the difficulty of determining their proper role. Feminists and others concerned with ethics of care express the concern that principlism gives primacy to moral norms rather than to interactions between people. Several student affairs scholars, including Upcraft and Poole (1991), believe that the specific principles outlined by Beauchamp and Childress (1994) do not have currency outside of the biomedical field. Assessing these and other problems with principles-based approaches to ethics will be a part of each chapter because *principlism* is a dominant practical ethics model.

Chapter Four: Case-Based Approaches to Ethics

Unlike a principles-based ethic, which has a more "top-down" or deductive approach to moral situations, case-based ethics focuses on the details of the case at hand. Case-based ethicists do not think that it is appropriate to take principles and impose them on a case; rather, as we analyze a situation, the guiding rules emerge from the facts of the case itself. This "bottom-up," or inductive, method asks questions like, *What are the particular elements of this situation and how should these shape my actions?* Two perspectives can inform the answer to this question: consequentialism and casuistry. Consequentialist reasoning looks to the future when assessing how an agent should act. Utilitarianism, one brand of consequentialism, uses the principle of utility to guide decision-making, asking *What action will produce the greatest good for the greatest number of people?* This theory operates from the perspective of a neutral observer who (allegedly) balances the interests of all relevant parties to produce more good than harm (Beauchamp & Childress, 1994). This future-oriented, consequentialist approach to moral reasoning is appealing because it provides a concrete method for incorporating concern for overall benefit into moral decision-making, a method particularly helpful in formulating policies. Utilitarianism also reminds us that the goal of moral reflection is maximizing the welfare of various constituents since sometimes this end is lost in moral deliberation (Beauchamp & Childress, 1994). Major criticisms of this version of consequentialism focus on the difficulty of predicting the future effects of actions and of determining which actors count as relevant parties. These elements will be investigated further in Chapter Four.

The second case-based theory we consider in Chapter Four is casuistry. This ancient approach fell into disrepute following various abuses during the Middle Ages and Renaissance, which eventually led to Blaise Pascal's famous critique in *The Provincial Letters* (1656/1967) but was reinvigorated by Albert Jonsen and Stephen Toulmin in their book *The Abuse of Casuistry: A History of Moral Reasoning* (1988). This approach orients moral reasoning to the past and tends to focus on a dialectical relationship between the case at hand and the knowledge gained from past experiences. Referring to precedents set in paradigmatic cases offers some guidance for navigating the current situation. This version of case-based reasoning is analogous to legal reasoning in that the precedents of previous cases form the main source of authority when deciding how to react to a current situation. Based on past experience, rules of thumb are developed to summarize some of the moral lessons that have been learned. Since these norms are grounded in experience, they are not universally applicable and are easily refined. One major difference between principles-based ethics and casuistry is the authority given to moral rules. For a casuist, the maxims that pertain to a given case are, at most, rules of thumb. These general action guides are dictated by the facts of the case and have minimal moral weight. Past experiences with similar situations allow us to reason analogically and see how rules functioned in those cases. If a rule that was helpful in one case does not seem appropriate in another case, however, no moral problem results from ignoring the rule.

Casuistry's primary emphasis on particular cases is very appealing for people who do not believe that rules provide adequate guidance in moral life. The problems with this method include the lack of consistent decision-making standards and the reliance on individuals to recognize when cases fit into a particular category. For example, when does a case about hanging a Confederate flag fall under *protection of the First Amendment* and not *preservation of good race relations*? In the ethics literature, much has been made of the alleged conflict between principles- and case-based approaches to ethics, a conflict captured succinctly by the question, *Are humans made for the law or the law for humans?* The contention seems to be that principles-based ethics are too removed from our everyday lives and that a case-based approach more adequately addresses the nuances of situations. In Chapters Three and Four, we work to dispel the insistence on a sharp separation of these approaches to ethics.

Chapter Five: Virtues-Based Approaches to Ethics

The first two approaches to ethics (i.e., principles-based and case-based) suppose that the purpose of ethics is to resolve problems. Principles-based ethics examines the moral norms in various situations, and case-based ethics focuses on the specifics of cases and how they shape our actions. Such conflict-oriented approaches to morality do not, however, pay sufficient attention to the character of the individual players in each case. In addition to considering the rules that apply to a situation and its particularities, virtues-based ethics injects the following questions into the mix: *What would be correct for me to do in light of my so-far-formed, and still forming, moral character?* (Pincoffs, 1971). *How does this action have an impact on the kind of person I want to be?* Unlike principles- and case-based approaches to ethics, virtues-based ethics is not focused on resolving conflicts but on the long-term impact of moral actions and consequences on the agent's character. Principles- and case-based approaches both play some role in routine circumstances, but each is oriented to crisis situations. "Agent-centered ethics [or virtue ethics], on the other hand, focuses on long term characteristic patterns of action, intentionally down-playing atomic acts and particular choice situations in the process" (Louden, 1984, p. 229). Not only does a virtues-based approach to ethics prescribe a different lens for viewing moral situations, it also uses a different form of reasoning for assessing the praise and blame due to the individuals involved. Decreasing the emphasis on specific individuals' acts also focuses increased attention on the importance of community in a virtues-based approach to ethics. In this chapter, we will examine briefly some of the communitarian critiques of principles- and case-based ethics and use this information to locate the passes existing between these moral mountains.

Virtue ethics accounts for the agents' character in moral situations and for the communities that shape their characters, but having roots in historical communities and focusing on agents and their virtues also leaves virtue ethics open to a wide array of criticisms. Many of these criticisms reveal significant gaps in a virtues-based approach to ethics, but they do not diminish the critical function such an approach can play in moral systems. We conclude Chapter Five by endorsing the integration of principles-, case-, and virtues-based ethics as the most complete approach to ethics in student affairs. Each method has various strengths and weaknesses that can be balanced by the other approaches.

Chapter Six: Conclusion: An Ethics of Responsibility

After you read Chapters Three through Five and the brief introduction they give to several major ethical theories, we ask you to ponder the following questions: *Which of the theories appeals to you the most? Do you have a preference among the theories, or do they all seem applicable in some situations? How would you describe the role that these theories play in your life? Can you describe the kinds of conflicts that may arise between someone who focuses on principles and someone who is more interested in virtues? Do you see these theories overlapping, or are they discrete and incommensurable?* Reading this text with these questions in mind will help keep you oriented as you encounter the ideas of these major approaches to ethics. Do not be dismayed if you read Chapter Three and find many parts of principlism appealing and then turn to Chapter Four and are equally persuaded of the value of a case-based approach. Most people draw from various ethical models for different purposes in their lives, and incoherence will not result from such a broad-based morality as long as you have an overarching guide for this process. This guide is your moral background, shaped by your family, ethnicity, religion, experiences, and other influences. Understanding your own moral values and framework will help identify the role ethics plays in your everyday life, and articulating your approach to ethics can help you identify points of tension when they arise. If you make decisions based on rules and policies while a co-worker emphasizes the particularities of the situation, serious disagreements can develop for which you need the language and background to understand the tension and its underlying roots.

In the last chapter, we will present an ethics of responsibility as one way to synthesize various approaches to ethics. In developing this approach, we draw on Margaret Urban Walker's expressive-collaborative approach to ethics, particularly its emphasis on our interconnectedness and the responsibilities this brings (Walker, 1998). The ethics of responsibility we present draws on the three ethics methods presented in the text, Walker's expressive-collaborative approach, and the contributions of feminism. While we find this framework helpful, we do not suggest that an ethics of responsibility is the only approach to ethics in student affairs administration. To reiterate, the objective of this book is to help you to identify which approaches to ethics reflect your personal values and to articulate the reasons behind this affinity.

We prefer a responsibility-based approach to ethics because it focuses on our longer-term relationships and the commitments that emerge from these interactions. We also appreciate the contributions of feminism, which help us uncover potential (or actual) power differentials among the people involved. Feminist ethics provides a critical tool with which we can examine social and cultural issues of oppression. By highlighting the patterns developed by traditionally male moral philosophers, feminist ethics shows us alternative ways to describe morality. Walker (1998) focuses on our relationships within our communities and the responsibilities inherent in these attachments. By combining multiple approaches to ethics in its fertile description of moral situations, responsibility-based ethics offers agents a variety of responses to a situation. Responsibility-based ethics entails a constant process of interpreting our relationships with other people and the commitments these relationships bring with them. The fluidity of this process requires a flexible approach to moral reflection that responds to the richness of our moral lives. For those familiar with the writing process, crafting a story, book, or poem involves some sense of where each character or theme is headed, but the process of writing itself often changes the initial conception of the story. Each of our lives is unfolding in many ways that we can or cannot control; moral evaluation of our lives is one way that we can try to understand the decisions we make and the people we are becoming. Reflection on morality is a dynamic process and should leave plenty of room for creative decisions that may not be produced by a single approach to morality.

The personal, responsive nature of responsibility-based and feminist ethics points to one of the major criticisms: these approaches to ethics are too subjective and relativistic and, therefore, have no place in public morality. A second major criticism involves their apparent inability to solve problems that arise. In Chapter Six, we will show that part of an ethics of responsibility is the adoption of the specific rules or laws for a given culture, and adherence to them is part of our individual responsibilities. If you have been raised in a Christian household in a Western culture, a large part of your personal responsibilities will include moral expectations that are drawn from that culture. While this approach is more flexible than others, it is not devoid of moral standards by which agents can be evaluated. When the values of specific societies conflict with our sense of personal responsibilities, feminist ethics offers us a mechanism for challenging rules that may not reflect our moral values. Whether we obey the rules or not (and why) is another part of our personal stories that may contribute very interesting information to any process of moral evaluation. An ethics of responsibility embraces this uncertainty while maintaining specific understandings of how we ought to treat other people. This approach to ethics allows for the mystery in life yet does not destroy other signposts that can guide us through life.

REFERENCES

Barr, M. J., & Associates (Eds.). (1993). *Handbook of student affairs administration*. San Francisco, CA: Jossey-Bass.

Beauchamp, T., & Childress, J. F. (1994). *Principles of biomedical ethics* (4th ed.). NY: Oxford University Press.

Canon, H. J., & Brown, R. D. (Eds.). (1985). *Applied ethics in student services*. (New Directions for Student Services, no. 30). San Francisco: Jossey-Bass.

Chambers, T. S. (1994, Spring). The bioethicist as author: The medical ethics case as rhetorical device. *Literature and Medicine, 13*, 60-78.

Chickering, A.W., & Reisser, L. (1993). *Education and identity* (2nd edition). San Francisco: Jossey-Bass.

Clouser, K. D., & Gert, B. (1990). A critique of principlism. *The Journal of Medicine and Philosophy, 15*, 219-236.

Elliott, C. (1992, July-August). Where ethics comes from and what to do about it? *Hastings Center Report, 22*(4), 28-35.

Fried, J. (Ed.) (1997). *Ethics for today's campus: New perspective on education, student development, and institutional management.* (New Directions for Student Services, no. 77). San Francisco: Jossey-Bass.

Gilligan, C. (1981). Moral Development. In A.W. Chickering & Associates (Eds.), *The modern American college* (pp. 139-157). San Francisco: Jossey-Bass.

Gilligan, C. (1993). *In a different voice: Psychological theory and women's development.* Cambridge, MA: Harvard University Press.

Jonsen, A. R., & Toulmin, S. (1988). *The abuse of casuistry.* Berkeley, CA: University of California Press.

Kitchener, K. S. (1984). Intuition, critical evaluation and ethical principles: The foundation for ethical decisions in counseling psychology. *Counseling Psychologist, 12*(3), 43-55.

Kitchener, K. S. (1985). Ethical principles and ethical decision making in student affairs. In H. J. Canon & R. D. Brown (Eds.), *Applied ethics in student services* (pp. 17-29). San Francisco: Jossey-Bass.

Louden, R. B. (1984, October) On Some Vices of Virtue Ethics. *American Philosophical Quarterly 21*, 227-236.

Nash, R. J. (1996). Fostering moral conversations in the college classroom. *Journal on Excellence in College Teaching, 7*(1), 83105.

Nash, R. J. (1997). Teaching ethics in the student affairs classroom. *NASPA Journal, 35*, 3-19.

Pascal, B. (1875). *The Provincial Letters.* (T. M'Crie, Trans.) London: Chatto and Windus. (Original work published 1656)

Pascarella, E. T., & Terenzini, P. T. (1981). *How college affects students.* San Francisco: Jossey-Bass.

Pincoffs, E. (1971). Quandary ethics. *Mind, 80*, 552-571.

Upcraft, M. L., & Poole, T. G. (1991). Ethical issues and administrative policies. In P. L. Moore (Ed.) *Managing the political dimension of student affairs* (pp. 81-93). San Francisco: Jossey-Bass.

Walker, M.U. (1998). *Moral understandings: A feminist study in ethics.* NY: Routledge.

CHAPTER ONE

Ethics and Student Affairs Administration

Ethics is a field that helps us to answer questions like *What is the most appropriate response in a given situation?* Morality provides a standard for conduct, character formation, and for life. (See p. 10, below, for a discussion of the distinction between *ethics* and *morality*.) Together with what we believe about ourselves, our situation, and the world, morality determines how we should act or shape ourselves (Frankena, 1980). Part of morality includes knowing the specific skills for resolving a conflict, but ethics also responds to questions about how to treat other people under more routine circumstances. Learning how to manage crises is an important component of ethics in student affairs, but ethics should also focus on everyday interactions. Ethics provides various methods for assessing the attitudes, actions, and values of professionals; revealing these roots can provide a necessary tool for understanding our actions in routine and antagonistic situations. How would you, for example, handle a situation in which a student sues you for violating his right to free speech? When handed a newspaper announcing that you are being sued, your response depends in part on your ethics. Would you be inclined to snap at your secretary, graciously retreat into your office, or faint? After reading this text, we hope you will have further developed the following skills and knowledge:

1. the ability to determine the quality of arguments for specific moral views;
2. a basic understanding of several major approaches to ethics;

3. the capacity to use this knowledge to identify moral issues in situations; and
4. the tolerance to appreciate multiple sides of a position or different approaches to ethics (Rosen & Caplan, 1980, pp. 30-31).

Ideally, a text like this will become unnecessary because a student affairs professional will gain the necessary moral reasoning skills to navigate through a variety of mountain ranges without an external guide.

CRISIS-ORIENTED ETHICS AND EVERYDAY ETHICS

To further the development of everyday ethics in student affairs, the authors explore several major ethical theories and, in doing so, outline a process that can help student affairs practitioners develop a language to describe their own approaches to morality. Harry Canon (1985) notes that Karen Kitchener's early work on principles in student affairs helped build this foundation of a common language, but we hope to expand upon this base and suggest other approaches to ethics for people who do not find Kitchener's model helpful. This text departs from most of the literature in the field of student affairs that considers ethics by placing a greater emphasis on everyday ethics. Most of the work on ethics in student affairs deals with the role of ethics in conflicts; this approach is indirectly suggested by the placement of the chapter on ethics in *The Handbook of Student Affairs Administration* (Barr, 1993). In this fundamental text, Harry Canon's chapter on ethics falls between Don G. Creamer's chapter "Conflict Management Skills" and Marsha A. Duncan's chapter "Dealing with Campus Crises." Although this anecdotal evidence is not proof that ethics has been accorded an unbalanced treatment in the student affairs literature, part of the task of this monograph is to dispel the perceptions created by such associations with conflicts and crises. In the case we present, a lawsuit brought against several student affairs professionals is only one part of a very complicated situation. Looking back at this crisis, we ask: *What was the climate on the campus that gave rise to this situation? How did the administrators and student leaders initially interact with the students who brought the lawsuit?*

Focusing on crises limits the role for ethics in our lives in the same way that focusing on one aspect of student life at a university can constrain the institution's potential for growth. Despite the commitment of the student affairs movement to developing *the whole student*, Terenzini, Pascarella, and Blimling (1996) describe a more dualistic "division of educational labor." Traditionally, faculty members and academic professionals are expected to promote students' academic and cognitive growth, while student affairs professionals are charged with enhancing students' affective growth. Attempts to introduce a broader understanding of student learning have led to the development of formal statements like *The Student Learning Imperative* (American College Personnel Association, 1994). In this document, student affairs professionals are charged with fostering conditions that enhance student learning and development and contribute to their institutions' academic missions. Since much research indicates that students develop holistically and that change in one area of their lives affects other areas, student affairs professionals assume a great deal of responsibility as they attempt to influence student development (Terenzini, Pascarella, & Blimling, 1996, p. 149). Given this responsibility and the potential for creating positive and negative experiences in students' lives, the field of student affairs administration requires constant internal and external evaluation. One mechanism for evaluating the *systems* enacted in student affairs divisions is research on outcomes, but since individual student affairs professionals associate directly with students, methods for evaluating these interactions are equally important. In this monograph, ethics is presented as an approach that encourages student affairs professionals to reflect on their professional and personal roles in higher education.

Higher education institutions are vast, complex webs consisting of many different threads of ethical interactions. Among the multiple ways that we interact with others on a daily basis are person-to-person, person-to-committee, person-to-institution, and institution-to-community encounters. Dealing with a student group's executive committee requires different skills from those employed in one-to-one discussions with students. Each situation presents challenges, not necessarily problems, that require careful attention. Shifting away from conceptions of ethics that focus on problems serves several purposes. First and foremost, attending to the ethics component of our everyday lives helps us see that ethics is not just another mechanism for assessing praise or blame in a situation. Understanding how ethics is embedded in the pattern of our daily encounters will make us more comfortable with its methods, and this heightened comfort will assist us when we do face conflicts. Some situations compel us to make judgments, such as when the safety of the other students is jeopardized. Ethics can contribute much more to this discussion than merely providing a tool for discipline or for a kinder and gentler way to tell co-workers and students that they made a mistake. The approach to ethics presented here is far more concerned with uncovering the way to evaluate situations than with determining who acted unethically. Ethics can help us formulate questions, e.g., *What factors in our community gave rise to this behavior?* or *How does our relationship with this person influence the way in which we attempt to change her actions?* Seeing ethics as a process to facilitate communication and set standards for our conduct gives a common language that is useful both in everyday and crisis settings.

In addition to shifting from a legal sense of ethics, a focus on everyday ethics can help define individual relationships with students and colleagues. Taking a stance on major issues is clearly an important part of any job; equally important, however, are the day-to-day interactions with a secretary or advisee, interactions that define us as professionals as much as, if not more than, our positions on issues like affirmative action or cohabitation in residence halls. We can observe this reality in action in any institutional committee. When studying a topic like student safety, the person convening the committee could select any number of participants. Individuals' interests and views on safety play some part in the decision, but so do judgments about whether a person is cooperative, respectful, and reliable (and political factors also influence the decisions). *Do we treat those around us with respect and fairness? Do our decisions seem arbitrary and a mere assertion of our power?* In the case outlined here, such judgments have a great impact on the course of events. Part of the difficulty with questions about our professional character is that we, as student affairs administrators, face the challenge of defining the kind of professionals we want to be in an ever-changing environment. At an obvious level, higher education environments change every year because one of their main purposes is to help students to graduate. Although the needs of students remain relatively stable, great variations arise in the issues presented by different years and generations of students. Students are being raised in cultures very different from the ones experienced by many student affairs professionals, and this too presents challenges. Balancing the ability to adapt to the changing needs of students with the need to remain relatively consistent when working with colleagues is not an easy task. Managing the multiple roles of the student affairs professional requires a process of reflection to guide decision-making in a variety of realms.

THREE MORAL MOUNTAINS

One way to organize our reflections on morality involves delineating three basic orientations to ethics; although these orientations are not mutually exclusive, each focuses more heavily on one area than the others. These three perspectives look at the agents involved, the actions being considered, and the circumstances surrounding these actions. Clearly, all three elements interact and influence each other, but separating them can help shed some light on various moral theories.

	Agent-Oriented	**Action-Oriented**	**Circumstances-Oriented**
Theories	Virtues-based ethics, character	Principles-based ethics, deontology and principlism	Case-based ethics, consequentialism and casuistry
Emphasis	Agents character: "Being a good person"	Moral rules and duties: "Doing the right thing according to moral principles"	Particularities of the situation: "Doing the right thing according to the circumstances at hand."

These general orientations to ethics do not completely encapsulate the theories we suggest to illustrate them. For example, principles-based approaches to ethics are also concerned with the particularities of situations and sometimes sanction the violation of a rule in the name of good consequences. These theories overlap in many areas but generally are distinguished from each other by their core features. To offer a brief example of how the three approaches to morality work, consider the case of dual relationships: a dean and graduate intern start dating while the student is under the dean's supervision. From an agent-oriented moral perspective, several reasons suggest that the dean is not demonstrating a virtuous character. First, her decision to date a student shows a lack of judgment (lack of the virtue prudence) since her university has a policy against such relationships. Also, she may be acting unfairly (lack of the virtue justice) by giving advantages to the student she is dating that are not offered to other students. Or perhaps it could be said that this dean is showing courage by violating a policy in the name of her love for the student. Essentially, virtues-based ethics is concerned with the agent and the way her acts reflect and shape her character.

A second approach to this situation would be based strictly on principles. For the purposes of this monograph, the terms *principles* and *rules* are generally used interchangeably since both are moral norms that guide our actions. Usually, principles have a more general construction than rules; this point will be probed in greater depth in Chapter Three. Some philosophers, like Immanuel Kant (1785/1981), view ethics as a duty-based, or deontological, approach. For them, it is primarily concerned with the nature of acts themselves and not with their consequences or the agents' motives. From this perspective, dating students is inherently wrong and the university's policy regarding this act is quite clear. The nature of the act itself, dating students, is wrong, regardless of the specific circumstances of the case or the character of the agent. Although deontological theories stress rules, "What is fundamental, in fact, are actions themselves and their moral properties" (Solomon, 1995, p. 739).

In contrast to such a principles-based approach, a case-based ethicist would address the specific characteristics of the case. Given the particularities of the case, perhaps the relationship is morally acceptable. If the dean is not favoring the student over other students, the dean and the student are quite close in age and are in love, and the student does not feel that he is suffering because of the relationship, then the positive aspects of their dating may outweigh the potential harm. The rule against dating students may be waived in this case, given the mitigating factors presented. In this approach to ethics, rules are mere guidelines for action, but the circumstances of the situation can easily provide justification for overriding the rule.

With these three elements of the situation in mind, try to answer the following questions: *Do you tend to pay more attention to the nature of the agent, the actions, or the circumstances in particular situations? Does your moral emphasis fall primarily on identifying moral character, adhering to principles, or maximizing good outcomes based on specific factors related to the case?*

Any discussion of ethics runs the risk of becoming too theoretical and abstract, so we have tried to limit our explorations to those topics that have direct relevance to student affairs. As Margaret Barr and M. Lee Upcraft (1990) have stated,

> *We cannot afford to let ethical statements and ethical practice remain abstract concepts. A commitment to ethical and responsible behavior provides the essential framework to guide our behavior in the future and aids us in approaching that future with optimism. (p. 17)*

Re-orienting ethical discussions to bring into focus the morality of everyday interactions will help realign the role ethics does and should play in our professional lives.

AN OVERVIEW OF PRACTICAL ETHICS

Before assessing the individual mountains on the horizon, we offer some background on the field of ethics. One should distinguish between *descriptive* and *prescriptive* ethics. Historians and sociologists employ the methods of descriptive ethics to study the beliefs and practices of different groups (Beauchamp & Childress, 1994, p. 5). Descriptive ethics helps us to reframe and evaluate one-on-one encounters between individuals, interactions between various groups on campus, and relations between higher education institutions and communities. For example, descriptive ethics can help us understand the dynamics between administrators and students that lead to the tension in the case, "Do Your Part." The culture of the university and the particular personalities of the people involved combined to create a complex situation. Using descriptive ethics to understand the values expressed in these relationships is a large part of our undertaking, but we are also concerned with prescriptive ethics. While descriptive ethics seeks to relate how things *are*, prescriptive ethics makes statements about how particular standards and values *should* shape our behavior. In the case we present, prescriptive ethics allows us to ask: *How should the students express their discontent with the current policy?* and *How should the administrators react to students openly breaking a university policy?* Our practical ethic makes use of both approaches: descriptive ethics in student affairs reveals underlying values and assumptions that are exposed to prescriptive ethics for analysis, assessment, and critical reflection.

Viewing a given field using the methods and concepts of ethics provides a "corrective lens." William F. May, a renowned ethicist at Southern Methodist University, writes,

Ethics relies heavily on the distinction between what is and what ought to be. Such corrective vision, however, challenges not so much the world the descriptive sciences see as the world distorted through the bias of institutional structures or through the prism of human imperfection and vice. (1983, pp. 13-14)

Given the complexity of contemporary universities and colleges, having tools to analyze the biases of institutional structures can help the student affairs profession to actively shape its evolution.

One example of this kind of reshaping is the tremendous change in the culture of medicine since the 1960s. In the last 25 years, bioethics has emerged as a field that provides an effective lens that reveals some of the overlooked areas in medicine. Prior to this, medicine lacked a consistent method for evaluating the relationship between physicians and patients or the impact of vast health care networks on the provision of care. The power structure of medicine depended so heavily on the expertise of the physician that little attention was given to the impact of illnesses and their therapies on the lives of patients. Bioethics arose in response to abuses of this professional power and as a remedy for undesirable patterns in physician-patient interactions. The bioethics literature provides varied perspectives on medical ethics as well as reflections on the limits of such ethics. Given the rich and vast literature of bioethics as a practical ethic (in its many permutations), the resources of the field can be quite useful.

We choose to draw from the experience of the development of practical bioethics for several reasons. First and foremost, *practical* as distinct from *theoretical* ethics took root and flourished in the health care environment and continues to expand. Although the concerns of practical ethics existed long before the advent of bioethics, the current explosion of interest in the former can be attributed, in part, to the success of the latter. Many of its early scholars drew extensively on classical philosophical and religious materials in order to shed light on some of the chronic issues in medicine. They adapted classical approaches to *ethics* and *morality* in order to work with the practical and concrete concerns of health care providers and patients. Although it is not always reflected in everyday discourse, philosophers and theologians draw a technical distinction between ethics and morality. Morality is one kind of action guide, a way that we shape our interactions with the world. This life guide includes norms and virtues, among other things, that help us formulate responses to specific people and things. Ethics functions at a different level from morality in that it seeks to answer broader, more theoretical questions, like "What is good?" or "What is virtue?" (Frankena, 1980, p. 4). Morality addresses *how* we should act while ethics analyzes *why* we maintain particular moral norms. While the meta-level of discourse is quite interesting, it is not the focus of this book. Since we are looking at practical ethics in student affairs administration, we will use the terms *ethics* and *morality* interchangeably.

In broad terms, morality seeks to help us answer the question, *How should I live and interact with other people?* Part of this question concerns particular values that help us define our conduct and mold our experiences. The phrase *applied ethics* is sometimes used to refer to the incorporation of ethics theory in areas such as student affairs, medicine, nursing, business, and environmental studies. Many bioethicists, including Beauchamp and Childress (1994), do not think the term *applied ethics* appropriately describes the way ethics can enrich the dialogue in these fields. *Applied ethics* suggests that tools from one field of expertise are being used in or even imposed on another field. While some critics may feel that this is the case, we do not. Ethics is woven into the fabric of all human relationships, including interactions that occur in professional environments. Conversely, the phrase *practical ethics* captures the sense that ethics is grounded in the *praxis* of student affairs, medicine, or business, rather than being injected by outsiders. For example, some administrators see their role as shaping, implementing, and enforcing university policies. Other administrators stress the development of relationships with students and give priority to these relationships over policy considerations. Rather than imposing a new ethical model, this monograph gives voice to some of the practical concerns of ethics in the daily business of student affairs administrators.

PRACTICAL ETHICS IN STUDENT AFFAIRS

We cannot stress strongly enough that we will be drawing on the *methods* used in bioethics, not the *substance* of the application of these methods to the field of medicine. Virtues-based ethics (agents), principles-based ethics (actions), and case-based ethics (circumstances) have histories far pre-dating and exceeding the scope of bioethics. For example, the Ten Commandments exemplify principles-based ethics. Although rules presented in more modern philosophical systems do not necessarily originate in a divinity (although sometimes they are treated as such), they share a basic moral orientation with the Ten Commandments. We draw on the ways that these approaches are used in the practical field of bioethics in order to learn from the successes and mistakes already made in explaining their function in concrete settings. We are not attempting to equate the issues of medicine with student affairs administration or to import the issues and language from medicine. Greater attention to the impact of methodological assumptions present in the bioethics literature may help us avoid some of the pitfalls associated with such cross-fertilization.

For example, M. Lee Upcraft and Thomas G. Poole (1991) have criticized Karen S. Kitchener's work with its five principles drawn from biomedical ethics (largely from Beauchamp and Childress (1994) and Paul Ramsey (1970)). They contend that the values of biomedical ethics are not universally applicable and thus do not translate well into the concerns of student affairs. Although we will address this issue in greater detail in Chapter Three, we would like to note that the problems that Upcraft and Poole find with the importing of principles from bioethics to student affairs are actually problems inherent in principles-based approaches to ethics. Every criticism leveled at the limitations of the principles in student affairs (but attributed to the fact that they come from bioethics) is also present in the bioethics literature. By looking at the pitfalls of various ethical theories, we feel confident that we can learn from scholars working in bioethics. Our task is to show that these approaches to ethics are intrinsically present in student affairs work. We are not trying to impose a model from another field on student affairs; rather, we intend to elucidate the ethics of the everyday in higher education settings.

Our approach is different from a professional code of ethics, which sets standards of behavior for members of a field but does not comment on the way that such rules fit into the daily lives of professionals. As Upcraft and Poole point out,

> *Ethical codes ... help to outline the boundaries of acceptable professional behavior. They remind us to be good people and responsible professionals and indicate some ways in which we can achieve those goals. However, professional codes of conduct give very little guidance for the solving of conflicts. Rather than helping us to answer our questions about moral conduct, they help us to raise more questions. (1991, p. 84)*

Given the limitations of professional codes in everyday and conflict-oriented ethics, we present an approach that offers a richer and more nuanced discussion of both aspects of ethics. Although we do not answer the student affairs professionals' questions concerning moral conduct, we propose a process that they can use to produce answers appropriate to their moral beliefs and to given situations (see the Introduction for this process). Sometimes the business of everyday life generates great conflicts or ethical dilemmas, the acceptable resolution of which requires skillful attention. We will provide some guidance for resolving these conflicts but believe strongly in the model of *preventive ethics*. As philosopher Edmund Pincoffs comments, "The moral philosopher can be thought of as prescribing a regimen for a healthy moral life rather than a cure for particular moral illnesses" (Pincoffs, 1971, p. 554). Gaining some perspective on how ethics functions in our everyday lives can go a long way toward preventing the damage that accompanies prolonged conflicts.

In order to maintain a balance in our moral lives, we must become aware of the values that guide our lives. Upcraft and Poole suggest an interesting model whose significance "lies in its ability to teach us about the origins of our moral problems" (Upcraft & Poole, 1991, p. 91). They present a twofold framework to assist in the identification of moral problems in student affairs: a vertical axis represents the management versus leadership roles of student affairs professionals, while a horizontal axis addresses individual versus communal needs. Upcraft and Poole's understanding of ethics can help individuals locate the origins of moral problems, but their proposed model is too limiting. One model cannot address the incredible diversity in the moral beliefs of student affairs professionals. While the virtues and values Upcraft and Poole suggest in their "Conceptual Framework for Ethics" may resonate with the moral concerns of some people, others may find them lacking.

The Upcraft and Poole model synthesizes many components of ethics that are usually treated as discrete entities, such as virtues and rules, but their approach falls short because it focuses largely on the ability of ethics to solve problems. Their main criticism of Kitchener's work with ethics is that it "stops short of helping to decipher many administrative dilemmas that pit the political against the ethical" (Upcraft & Poole, 1991, p. 85). While we support efforts to draw together traditionally separate approaches to ethics, we do not find it helpful to focus solely on the role of ethics in solving problems to the exclusion of its other aspects. We build upon Upcraft and Poole's attempt to design an ethical framework that identifies the origins of moral problems, and we construct a process that helps student affairs administrators identify their moral frameworks in everyday life. Addressing conflicts may be part of this framework, but it certainly does not exhaust ethical activity. Since we view ethics as a part of every interaction, a part that ideally informs these encounters, we do not believe that the endorsement of an "ethics professional or officer" is necessary at any higher education institution (Barr & Golseth, 1990, p. 209). Understanding ethics as underlying all human relations helps to dispel notions that ethics is imposed on the field by outside experts. Equipping individuals with the skills to recognize the ethical components of their everyday activities will help them resolve conflicts as they arise. We will begin this process in Chapter Three with an exploration of a major principles-based method in ethics.

REFERENCES

American College Personnel Association [ACPA]. (1994). *The student learning imperative: Implications for student affairs.* Washington, DC: Author.

Barr, M. J., & Associates (Eds.). (1993). *Handbook of student affairs administration.* San Francisco: Jossey-Bass.

Barr, M. J., & Upcraft, M. L. (Eds.). (1990). *New futures for student affairs.* San Francisco: Jossey-Bass.

Barr, M. J. & Golseth, A. E. (1990). Managing change in a paradoxical environment. In M. J. Barr & M. L. Upcraft (Eds.), *New futures for student affairs* (pp. 201-216). San Francisco: Jossey-Bass.

Beauchamp, T., & Childress, J. F. (1994). *Principles of biomedical ethics* (4th ed.). NY: Oxford University Press.

Canon, H. J., & Brown, R. D. (Eds.). (1985). *Applied ethics in student services.* (New Directions for Student Services, no. 30.) San Francisco: Jossey-Bass.

Canon, H. J. (1993). Maintaining high ethical standards. In M. J. Barr & Associates (Eds.), *The handbook for student affairs administration* (pp. 327-339). San Francisco: Jossey-Bass.

Frankena, W. (1980). *Thinking about morality.* Ann Arbor, MI: University of Michigan Press.

Kant, I. (1981). *Grounding for the metaphysics of morals* (J.W. Ellington, Trans.) Indianapolis, IN: Hackett. (Original work published in 1785)

May, W. F. (1983). *The physician's covenant: Images of the healer in medical ethics.* Philadelphia, PA: Westminster Press.

Pincoffs, E. (1971). Quandary ethics. *Mind, 80,* 552-571.

Ramsey, P. (1970). *The patient as person; Explorations in medical ethics.* New Haven: Yale.

Rosen, B., & Caplan, A. L. (1980). *Ethics in the undergraduate curriculum.* Hastings-on-Hudson, NY: The Hastings Center.

Solomon, W. D. (1995). Ethics: Normative ethical theories. In W. T. Reich (Ed.) *Encyclopedia of bioethics* (Rev. ed., Vol. 2, pp. 736-748). NY: Macmillan.

Terenzini, P. T., Pascarella, E. T., & Blimling, G. S. (1996). Student's out-of-class experiences and their influences on learning and cognitive development: A literature review. *Journal of College Student Development, 37,* 149-162.

Upcraft, M. L., & Poole, T. G. (1991). Ethical issues and administrative policies. In P. L. Moore (Ed.) *Managing the political dimension of student affairs* (pp. 81-93). San Francisco: Jossey-Bass.

CHAPTER TWO

Do Your Part

with H. Samuel Miller and Laurence G. Mueller

Editor's Note: The following case is based on an actual situation. The names and some of the facts have been changed. The quotations are based on actual statements from interviews with the participants in the case.

PART A - ESTABLISHING THE TRADITION

Background

It was the first week of November, two months into school at Old State University [OSU], and Laura McMahan, Associate Dean of Students, was concerned about the growing controversies between the Resident Staff and residents in Forman Residential College, just beginning its second year. It had been a busy fall, but she thought she knew the status of most of the situations in the residential areas. As she headed to her weekly staff meeting in the Dean of Students Office, Laura thought about what she needed to accomplish before the end of the day. She could not have anticipated that within minutes she would be served with a restraining order.

The University

Laura McMahan's institution, a highly selective university of 17,000 students (11,500 undergraduates), was founded on the principles of training citizens for public service and active participation in the democratic process. Since its inception, OSU's curriculum had always offered a broader and more diverse scope of study than other colleges. The founder supported ideas of religious freedom and student self-governance. These permeated the culture of the institution and still do to this day. The concept of an intellectual and spiritual environment where faculty and students lived and worked together constituted the university's basic philosophy beginning in the early 1800s and continued to govern modern day residential areas, which housed almost 5,200 students.

Residential Living

Consistent with the founding philosophy of OSU, the organizational structure that governed the residential areas was highly dependent on the participation of student leaders. Three full-time student affairs professionals—two Assistant Deans of Students (Betty Dickinson and Wayne Chester) and one Associate Dean of Students (Laura McMahan)—supervised approximately 180 undergraduate students and 20 graduate students who held positions as Resident Staff members. The staff of 200 supervised, managed, and voted on policies for the nearly 5,200 students living in university housing. The Resident Staff had within its own body a decision-making group known as the Executive Committee. This group comprised all of the student hall or house directors and was led by two undergraduate chairpersons. The chairpersons of the Resident Staff program were university spokespersons for the residential areas and were supervised by the Assistant and Associate Deans of Students. All of the positions on Resident Staff were highly sought after, and its members were considered to be university-wide student leaders. Resident Staff members participated in a variety of committees throughout the university and were well-respected for their feedback regarding the residential life system.

Forman Residential College

Based on suggestions from student leaders around the campus, the Vice President for Student Affairs, the Provost, and the Executive Vice President for Budget and Finance [the Steering Committee] appointed a committee to evaluate how students were housed at the university and to plan ways to make improvements. After extensive study, the committee recommended that a residential area housing 280 sophomores, juniors, and seniors be developed into a program of living called *a residential college*. The plan called for the students' living experience to contribute actively to their physical, ethical, and intellectual development. To flesh out its plan for a residential college, the Steering Committee evaluated various aspects of the living experience in university housing, with the goal of deciding whether the environments stimulated and guided the student in a broad range of activities. The Steering Committee assessed academic, extracurricular, cultural, athletic, and social activities, as well as special forms of counseling and assistance where appropriate. The primary functions of the residential programs were evaluated according to whether they promoted in the students and in the faculty a more comprehensive concern for the students' entire educational development. The committee's plan recommended providing residential areas where faculty members and students would live, dine, and interact together. The first area designated for improvement was Forman College.

Based on the committee's assessments, an organizational structure and program were developed by a subcommittee of the Steering Committee, made up of faculty, students, and administrators. The residential college organizational structure and governing body were created primarily by student Resident Staff members from the Executive Committee of Resident Staff. The basic elements of a residential college included: a) common dining; b) faculty participation through both a faculty fellows program and administrative responsibility for the college; c) academic programs; and d) an internal student governance system. These elements were supported by two faculty members who assumed administrative responsibilities and lived within the college, as well as two other faculty members who lived among the students for daily interaction. The Steering Committee successfully recruited highly regarded teaching faculty members for these positions. In addition to the administrative oversight, the residential college, as part of the university residential life system, was supported by the Resident Staff program. Five student staff members lived in the college and were supervised directly by a hall director, who was also a student. The staff members received additional support from the deans of students working with the residential areas. The Resident Staff members who were placed in Forman were selected through a centralized university process that included an additional interview for placement in Forman. The faculty and students of Forman were involved in the interview process for the Resident Staff members.

The governance structure of Forman was proposed by the student Resident Staff members and included an executive leadership group with an extensive system of student committees. The students on these committees decided everything from membership and budget expenditures to educational and social programming. The Master of Forman College was a highly regarded tenured faculty member who at one point in his career was the Dean of the largest school at OSU. He also had been part of the university-wide development team for the new residential college system. The Dean of Instruction for the students in Forman likewise was a tenured faculty member with a strong reputation as a student advocate. During the first year of Forman College's operation, the Hall Director and two of the resident assistants were part of the team that had developed the college.

Developing Governance within Forman College

Having been instrumental in developing the new student governance structure, the Resident Staff who lived within the College were committed to its success. They realized that there would be many opportunities to foster the growth of this new community and help the students learn the university rules and policies within which the new government would need to exist. The College was designed so that the students would be highly involved in the daily activities and operation of the college. This plan proved to be very successful. The Resident Staff members who drafted the original structure made sure that students were involved in every aspect of its operation. For example, students applied to be members of Forman College by submitting an application that included two essays. During the first year, a team of faculty members, administrators, and student Resident Staff members spent their winter break selecting the residents for Forman. The process was established so that in future years a committee of Forman College residents would choose the new members. The students at OSU were seen as involved, respected, and possessed with an independence and love of intellectual discourse that exemplified the founding spirit of OSU.

The academic year 1986-1987 saw the opening of Forman Residential College, which went very smoothly. A few weeks after the opening, elections for the student governance system took place. The whole Residential College community elected a President, Vice-President, and Treasurer. They presided over the Representative Council, on which one elected member represented each residence hall. With such an elected government, the Forman College students no longer saw a need for "interference" from Residence Life. It was known, however, that there would be five Resident Assistants who would live within the college because it was part of the University residential life system.

Soon after its election, the student government began defining both the rules and opportunities that would be available to residents. Tasks formerly accomplished by the Resident Staff, such as voting on security policies, organizing intramural activities, holding elections for residence hall representatives, and organizing social events, now were under the jurisdiction of the Forman College Student Government. The elected officials solicited nominations for appointed positions within the College and appointed co-chairs for each of the following committees: social, academic and cultural, membership, outreach and service, food and dining, intramurals, and historical. From the student perspective, once governance was relinquished to Forman College residents, oversight from Residence Life no longer was necessary. Students then viewed the Resident Staff as having the responsibility only of distributing and collecting keys and serving as surrogates for the University Police in enforcing University policy.

In spring 1987, the first Hall Director and most of her staff graduated, leaving a new Resident Staff who had not been a part of designing the original structure of Forman College. Helen Weber, the newly selected Hall Director, had been a member of the Resident Staff, however, and two of the Resident Assistants had been students within the College. The new Resident Staff had received training to lead and establish rules within all living environments, and they arrived at Forman to fulfill their mission. Immediately, the student government rebuffed them for overstepping the bounds of the College's governance structure. Many of the students in Forman College thought that the cooperative spirit and commitment of the Resident Staff in the College were gone.

Security in Residential Areas

One of the first issues that created conflict between the staff members and the students was a new security policy. Concern for safety and security within colleges and universities had risen nationally as cases of theft, rape, and even murder had occurred at institutions throughout the country. This knowledge of incidents taking place across the country, combined with the recommendations of the University Police and requests from parents, compelled the university to take a closer look at the security within the residential areas.

The design of the residential system at OSU consisted primarily of three- or four-story buildings that housed between 120 and 140 students each, with some of the buildings connected to others by enclosed hallways or tunnels. Each residence hall had several outside entrances, which usually were left unlocked, and keys were required for the hallway or room doors. In residential areas with apartments or suites, the outside door of each unit could be locked as could the individual room doors. Since each residence hall had several entrances, no central desk areas or personnel within the areas who handled security were set up; the only security personnel were Resident Staff members scattered throughout the living area. The University Police were considered competent and responsive but did not reside in the residential areas. The atmosphere of trust within the OSU academic community extended to the residential areas, and many students left their room doors open or propped outside doors.

Forman College and Security Issues

Conflict with Forman students quickly came to a head when the Resident Staff declared that all outside access doors to the College would be locked 24 hours a day. This decision was made by the student Executive Committee of Resident Staff, which governed all residential areas. The Office of Residence Life weighed in heavily on the decision to establish and enforce the 24-hour security policy. Laura McMahan indicated that it had been under consideration for a full year before any action was taken. Laura explained,

> *Compared nationally, I believed we could be considered as acting negligently concerning our lax security policies. We just had to make the change to the 24-hour security policy for the residents, because we knew they wouldn't do it on their own. We were fortunate that the Residence Staff Executive Committee supported the idea and agreed to enforce it.*

This flew in the face of the policy that the College's students had voted to establish the previous year that said that "doors would be locked from midnight until 8:00 a.m." For the 200 returning students of Forman, the decision from Residence Life violated the self-governance that was guaranteed by the constitution of the College. Residents felt that they had the unfettered right to run the College as they saw fit and that the new security policy infringed upon this right. Furthermore, the policy was seen as a severe inconvenience, because each student had a key to only one of the fourteen access doors (Exhibit 1). Therefore, residents would be forced to go to their specific access door to enter the complex, instead of using the connecting tunnels beneath the twelve residence halls. This caused varying degrees of inconvenience when the weather was unpleasant or the students wanted to visit a resident in another part of the complex. Students also indicated that the new policy would be isolating; friends not living in the College would have a difficult time gaining access to visit them.

At an early meeting that included the Resident Staff (co-chairs, deans, and Forman College Resident Staff) and the Forman College residents, the Resident Staff members argued that it was strictly a security issue to make sure the doors were always locked. Charles Graham, past-President of the College, countered, explaining,

> *If the doors are unlocked, a resident who was being chased could run inside any of the access doors, instead of having to run to their own access door and fumble for their keys. We have put in requests for security phones around the college, but there has been no action. We feel that having a greater number of police patrols in the area is a better answer than just locking everything down and isolating the community.*

Recognizing its lack of success in arguing with the Resident Staff, the Forman student government resorted to precedent. In freshman residence halls, a vote commonly was taken each year to determine the security hours for the year (See Exhibit 2). Although a vote would not be taken this year, the policy had been in operation when the students in Forman College were freshmen in the other residential areas. The Forman College student government

EXHIBIT 1 — LAYOUT OF FORMAN COLLEGE AT OLD STATE UNIVERSITY

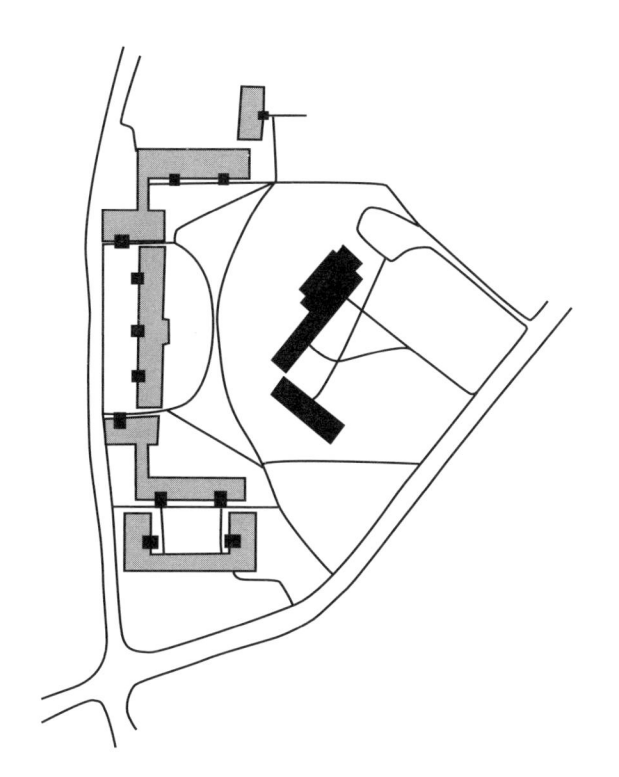

Gray Buildings: Forman College Residence Halls

Black Buildings: Forman College classrooms and faculty residences

Blocks: Denotes entrances to residence hall areas

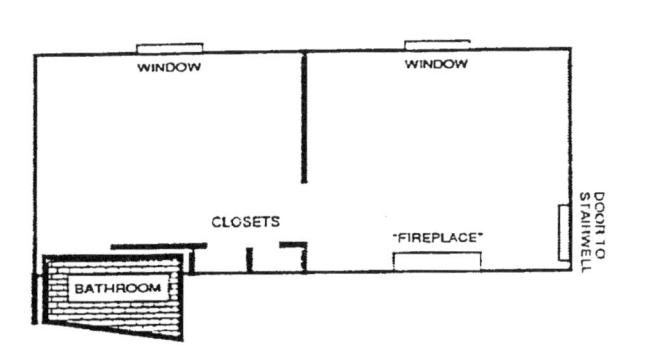

Typical floorplan for rooms in Forman College residence halls.

EXHIBIT 2 — SECURITY POLICIES FOR OLD STATE UNIVERSITY RESIDENCE HALLS

SECURITY POLICY

The reality that the University is not a separate community from the surrounding municipalities requires that appropriate security measures are taken in order to provide a safe environment for all residents. As noted in the goals and purposes of Resident Staff, Staff members are ultimately charged with informing their residents of their responsibility for maintaining a "comfortable and secure living area." In this endeavor:

1. Resident Staff members make residents aware of the potentially dangerous situations, and encourage <u>them</u> to take reasonable precautions; i.e., locking doors, avoid walking alone, close curtains while dressing, keep bicycles locked.

2. All Staff members, and especially the staff in charge of dorm security, should take responsibility for ensuring that all access doors are locked at 12:00 Midnight each night. ALL FIRE DOORS MUST BE CLOSED AND LOCKED AT ALL TIMES EXCEPT IN CASE OF EMERGENCY.

3. When a suspicious looking person is in the dorm area, the Staff member should confront that person and request an I.D. However, if the stranger appears very suspicious, Staff members should call the Police, and keep an eye on the suspect rather than confront the person.

4. Neither solicitations nor deliveries are permitted within the dormitory without the expressed written permission of the Office of the Dean of Students. Report any violation of this policy to the Office of Residence Life, and, if necessary call the University Policy.

5. Resident Staff members use Master Keys only in accordance with the guidelines established by the Office of Residence Life and the Housing Division.

6. Until Sunday, September 15, 1986, visitation will be allowed in the freshman dormitories as follows:
    Monday - Thursday   9:00 a.m. - Midnight
    Weekends   Open visitation until Sunday
                             at Midnight

Following this period, individual suites or halls must vote <u>by secret ballot</u> to establish visitation hours according to the majority of the group's wishes.

Upperclass residents will determine visitation hours <u>by secret ballot</u> according to the majority of the group's wishes.

rebuffed the newly imposed rules and proceeded to call a vote of the full College membership on the security hours. The vote came back with an overwhelming confirmation of the midnight until eight a.m. lock-up policy of the previous year. The Resident Staff said that in spite of the vote, "the access doors would remain locked 24 hours a day, as was decided by the Resident Staff Executive Committee." Helen Weber, the current Hall Director of Forman College, remembered when the Executive Committee of Resident Staff voted to lock all residence hall doors, including those in the freshman halls, 24 hours.

While I agreed [with the policy] I did not think the students would like it. I personally believed that it was the right thing since I had insider information to the problems and incidents reported to the judiciary committee. I also knew how easy it was to hide in the halls.

The decision to enforce the 24-hour security policy incited the student government to ask its members to voice their anger at having governance decisions removed from the student population. The college's student government forwarded petitions and complaints to the Assistant Dean of Students in Residence Life, Betty Dickinson (Exhibit 3). The Office of Residence Life upheld its decision to keep the 24-hour security system. Students in the College did not believe they were being heard, so they took their own action and began to keep the access doors from closing. These actions included throwing the door-chain over the top of the door, duct-taping the lock open, jimmying the panic-bar to remain open, propping the door open with a brick, and other more creative ideas. These actions were popular among many residents, providing the convenience of unlocked access doors and a way to fight back against the newly imposed rules. The Resident Staff members reacted by instituting patrols to close the doors properly and submitting written reports to Residence Life when students violated rules of conduct (Exhibit 4). As soon as a Resident Staff member would close a door, however,

EXHIBIT 3 — LETTER REGARDING FORMAN COLLEGE PETITION ON SECURITY POLICY

Forman College
Old State University

October 14, 1987

Ms. Betty Dickinson
Assistant Dean of Students - Upperclass Housing
Residence Life Office
Old State University

Dear Ms. Dickinson

Pursuant to the recent petition by the residents of Forman College regarding our security policy, on or about October 21st we will be taking a vote of the College to determine which hours we would like to have our entrance doors locked. Knowing that you have an interest in this matter, we invite you to address the College, in writing or in person, that you might share your point of view with us.

Should you care to address the College, our banquet on Wednesday the 21st would be a great opportunity. Though remarks are usually not extensive due to the entertainment schedule, we do have a period for announcements following the meal. Of course you are more than welcome to come for dinner.

We look forward to hearing from you.

Sincerely,

Charles Graham

EXHIBIT 4 — INCIDENT REPORT FROM FORMAN COLLEGE

Residence Life Program
SERIOUS INCIDENT REPORT

To be used by the Resident Staff and the Office of Residence Life when incidents of a serious nature occur in the dorm areas.

Type of Incident: (circle one) Crime, Fire Alarm, Housing, Medical, Psychological, Other _Crime_

Alcohol Related: YES ___ NO _X_

Submitted by: ▓▓▓▓▓▓▓▓▓▓ Dorm: ▓▓▓▓▓▓▓▓▓▓

Date Submitted: _10/15/87_

Date of Incident: _10/15/87_

Approximate Time of Incident: _12:00 p.m._

Name of Person(s) Involved in Incident: _Guilty party is unknown. Suspect is ▓▓▓▓▓._

Witness(es) to Incident: _None_

Resident Staff Description of Incident: _Push handle on portal door has been broken. Screws were removed from the panel containing the door lock. Other previous incidents: Sat. → glued dime in lock, Mon (another glued penny in lock), Wed → glued dime in lock, Thurs. → nail driven into lock._

If Medical Attention required, give details: _N/A_

If police called, give details: _Police department was notified at approximately 5:30. Event was described and officer was given the name of the suspect._

If University property damaged, give details: _▓▓▓▓ portal door lock is now completely broken and the push handle has been removed._

What action has been taken as a result of the incident? _The police department has been notified. (#22, ▓▓▓▓). RLO has also been notified as well._

FOLLOW-UP (to be completed by Office of Residence Life)
Date Received: _____ Referred to: _____
COMMENTS:

a sympathetic student would go back and prop it open again. It became a game. Despite these violations, all the Forman College residents would ensure that the doors were closed and locked before midnight, without the Resident Staff members' prompting. At this point, the relationship between the College student government and many of the student residents, and the Resident Staff who lived within the College was entirely adversarial.

Questions before further reading:
- *Who should determine the safety and security policies within a community?*
- *Should different rules apply within each residential community?*
- *What action, if any, should be taken?*

PART B - THE TRADITION DEVELOPS

While OSU was located in a charming and relatively safe city, it like the rest of the world was changing. Crime was widespread, and students increasingly were becoming the targets. The Resident Staff recognized this change and tried to make adjustments to keep pace. They felt that the new security policy was principled, well-reasoned, and justified. Formal discussions at an open forum were finally initiated between the College student government and Residence Life. At this forum, the co-chairmen of the Resident Staff discussed security reports, including a rape, which had occurred at the College (Exhibit 5). They followed the report with security figures about all the residence halls around the University, highlighting the College as having the highest number of incidents (Exhibit 6). Finally, they indicated that based upon this information, they had decided to impose the 24-hour security policy on all of the residential areas, including the College. One College resident shouted out, "You made this sweeping policy based on one rape! What about involving the student government system which has been established?" Resident Staff officials indicated that they were well within their right to change the rules

EXHIBIT 5 — FORMAN COLLEGE FIRE/POLICE SERVICE CALLS

OLD STATE UNIVERSITY
Department of Police

Office of the Director

The following is a total of calls for service to the Forman College dorms from the spring of 1983 to the present. There is a breakdown by the academic year and by offense type with totals for each year at the bottom of the form.

OFFENSE	Spr '83	83-84	84-85	85-86	86-87	Fall 87
Assault					1	
Robbery		1				
B&E		1				
Ind Exp		1				
Trespass			1		1	
Larceny	2	4	7	1	9	1
Vandalism		1	3	4		1
Prop Damage				1		
Lost Prop	1	1	3		3	
Found Prop		3	1			1
Disorder					1	
Susp Circ	1	5		2	4	2
Susp Pers	1	2	2	1	7	
Solicitor	1	1				
Annoy Calls			1		1	
Missing Pers		1			2	
Hazard	1					
Fire Alarm	2	5	8			
Assist Other Agency					1	1
TOTAL	9	27	27	9	30	6

EXHIBIT 6 — SECURITY POLICY STATISTICS

OLD STATE UNIVERSITY
Department of Police

Office of the Director

Memo To: Director M. York

From: Sgt. M. A. Dole

Subject: Police Responses to the Dorm Areas

The following firgures represent police responses to dormitory areas for the period of September 1 through November 3 for the academic years of 85-86, 86-87, and the current year.

	85-86	86-87	87-88
Assaults	1	3	1
Burglary (and attempts)	3	2	0
Larcenies (and attempts	50	31	8
Arson	1	0	0
Indecent Exposure	0	1	0
Vandalism	7	7	10
Trespassing	3	1	0
Disorders & Domestics	3	2	6
Drunk in Public	2	2	0
Fireworks	0	5	0
Annoying Phone Calls	0	3	0

There were also several miscellaneous categories that were not necessary criminal in nature or that fell in a "suspicious" category.

	85-86	86-87	87-88
Student Injuries	1	1	1
Fires/Alarms/Hazards	14	4	4
Suspicious Circumstances/People/Vehicles	55	38	14
Property Lost/Found/Accidental Damage	15	10	8
Noise Complaints	14	22	3
Miscellaneous Calls	15	16	2

and enforce the new ones. On the security issue, the University, the Office of Residence Life, and the Resident Staff members were of a single mind: one rape was one too many. They were prepared to take considerable heat because they believed that the new security policy was guaranteed to reduce thefts and improve safety.

The discussion portion of the forum ended abruptly, and only nonconstructive remarks followed. Mark Dally, a vocal resident, exclaimed, "You obviously don't care what we think." Prior to the meeting, College residents had not heard about the rape. They most certainly were concerned, and some residents were even very understanding of a suggested change in policy. Most still were upset, however, that the new security policy had been enacted by "outsiders," not by the residents who lived within the College.

Soon after the forum, Charles Graham, Mark Dally, and five other residents sat down together to discuss how Forman College residents could fight for their student governance rights. Mark explained to the others,

There are no other avenues to make ourselves heard but to advocate civil disobedience. No harm. No foul. We have tried informal discussions, formal forums, but nobody is listening to the decisions made by our Representative Council. We need to stir things up.

From this meeting the resistance grew more stalwart, and an underground press campaign was mounted to encourage students to prop the doors open. The Resident Staff's threats of punishment for propping open doors were constant. When the Resident Staff brought a student up on judiciary charges for removing and damaging his window screen, residents began to believe that the Resident Staff was looking for any reason to punish residents who might be supportive of door propping. Unfortunately, James Hill, the dedicated, hard-working maintenance man at the College, was caught between the two sides. James diligently fixed every mechanism used to keep the doors open, in accordance with his job responsibilities and orders from University Housing.

The grassroots door-propping campaign was propagated by posters within Forman College. Stapled to access doors were flyers satirically suggesting methods of ensuring that the access doors would not close (Exhibits 7, 8, and 9). Hours after these posters were put up, members of Resident Staff removed them. The Resident Staff claimed that these posters were posted illegally. Another batch of signs went up the same day, this time posted on the official Forman College bulletin boards. Again the Resident Staff tore down the posters. Mark Dally remembered, "We asked them nicely not to take them down; it was our right to protest. We were using the board properly, and there were many other things posted by outsiders on those boards which were much more profane and inciting." The Resident Staff claimed that the posters were stirring up the situation and promoting a violation of the new security rules. This time, following their removal, the same posters were put up again, accompanied by posters indicating that there were "forces at work," i.e., the Resident Staff, who were infringing on freedom of speech (Exhibits 10 and 11).

Helen Weber removed the first set of posters because they were placed improperly and they insulted James, who was very offended. She equated the posters with telling a murderer how to kill when he was in a state of murderous rage (which she understood to be against the law). When Helen called Dean Dickinson, the dean told her it had been Helen's decision, not Residence Life's, to take down the posters. Even though Dean Dickinson was correct, Helen felt completely hung out to dry. Later that day, Dean McMahan called Helen to apologize, explaining that Residence Life would support Helen and her staff but that the staff should stop taking down the posters. Helen explained that the staff had stopped taking down the posters when the students complained about their being removed. Helen remembered feeling isolated at the time:

> As the Hall Director of Forman College, I felt totally locked out of the process. The Deans were handling it, but we never got any information. When we asked, we were told it was being worked out.

EXHIBIT 7 — "WAYS TO KEEP YOUR DOOR UNLOCKED" POSTER

WAYS TO KEEP YOUR DOOR UNLOCKED

DUCT TAPE OVER LATCH
JAM LATCH WITH PAPER OR TWIG
BLOCK OPEN WITH HUGE LOG
BLOCK OPEN WITH HUGE BOULDER
USE R.A. AS A DOORSTOP
GIVE DAVE "THE MAINTENANCE MAN" A FIVE-SPOT
REMOVE DOOR (USE YOUR BEST JUDGEMENT)
FUN WITH SUPER GLUE (Ibid.)
DRAPE CHAIN OVER DOOR
PUT FOREIGN OBJECTS INTO DOORJAMB:
GUM
EPOXY BLOB
COINS
SMALL CHILDREN
SEX TOYS
ASSISTANT DEAN DICKINSON
GIVE LOCK PARTS TO PARENTS AS SOUVENIRS

DO YOUR PART

"THE OPPRESSED IN FORMAN COLLEGE, LIKE FREEDOM FIGHTERS EVERYWHERE, ARE IN THE HEARTS AND MINDS OF THE AMERICAN PEOPLE."
Lt. Col. Oliver North

EXHIBIT 8 — "STORY OF THE LOCK-DOWN" POSTER

THE STORY OF THE 24-HOUR LOCK-DOWN

LATE SPRING, 1987
A NEW RESIDENCE LIFE STUDENT LEADERSHIP SEARCHES FOR A WAY TO "MAKE THEIR MARK ON THE UNIVERSITY."

EARLY FALL, 1987
THIRTY-FIVE HEAD R.A.'S DECIDE FOR THE ENTIRE STUDENT BODY TO INSTITUTE AN ILL-CONCEIVED, DRASTIC 24-HOUR LOCK-DOWN.

OCTOBER 25, 1987
NEEDED COMPROMISES ARE DISCUSSED BY THIS EXECUTIVE COMMITTEE, BUT ARE DISCARDED ". . . SO THAT WE WON'T LOOK WISHY-WASHY." *ASSISTANT* DEAN DICKINSON QUASHES DIALOGUE OF THIS MATTER IN THE R.A. NEWSLETTER.

LATE FALL, 1987
STUDENTS BEGIN TO REALIZE THEIR VOICE IS NOT BEING HEARD!!!

"POWER COWWUPTS, AND ABSOWUTE POWER COWWUPTS ABSOWUTEWEY."
Elmer Fudd

DO YOUR PART

EXHIBIT 9 — "NEW AND IMPROVED" POSTER

New and Improved!!!

WAYS TO KEEP YOUR DOOR UNLOCKED

DUCT TAPE OVER LATCH
JAM LATCH WITH PAPER OR TWIG
BLOCK OPEN WITH HUGE LOG
BLOCK OPEN WITH HUGE BOULDER
USE R.A. AS A DOORSTOP
SMALL THERMONUCLEAR DEVICE
REMOVE DOOR (JUST KIDDING)
FUN WITH SUPER GLUE (Ibid.)
DRAPE CHAIN OVER DOOR
PUT FOREIGN OBJECTS INTO DOORJAMB:
GUM
EPOXY BLOB
COINS
ECUADORIAN SWEATERS
SMALL CHILDREN
SEX TOYS
EMPTY KEGS (OOPS)

"THE OPPRESSED IN FORMAN COLLEGE, LIKE FREEDOM FIGHTERS EVERYWHERE, ARE IN THE HEARTS AND MINDS OF THE AMERICAN PEOPLE."
Lt. Col. Oliver North

DO YOUR PART

EXHIBIT 10 — "FIRST AMENDMENT" POSTER

FIRST AMENDMENT ?????????????

DOES IT BOTHER YOU THAT POLITICAL LITERATURE IS BEING SUPPRESSED AT FORMAN COLLEGE?

TELL YOUR RESIDENT ASSISTANT TO STOP REMOVING FLYERS THAT EXPRESS OPINIONS CONTRARY TO THEIRS!!!!

"I MAY DISAGREE WITH WHAT YOU SAY, BUT I WILL DEFEND TO THE DEATH YOUR RIGHT TO SAY IT."
SEN. JOE BIDEN

DO YOUR PART

EXHIBIT 11— "DID YOU KNOW" POSTER

DID YOU KNOW
??????????????

OPPRESSION

Do you feel oppressed? Do you feel under siege? Do you feel like you live in a fortress?

If you've answered yes to any of these questions, you're not alone. Forman College residents this year are oppressed, under siege, and we all live in a fortress.

Fortunately, the intolerable status quo need not always be: gestapo RA's can be replaced; locked doors can be unlocked (or taken off); oppressive rules can be ignored.

DO YOUR PART!

Publius

END THIS SILLINESS!

NEXT THEY WILL WANT YOUR FIRST BORN!

POLITICAL PRISONERS? MOSCOW OR FORMAN?

There are presently 8 Forman College residents being singled out by the powers that be for an alleged crime, but they are denied the courtesy of a most basic human right, the right to know the exact nature of the allegation made against them.

They are being threatened and bullied into a coerced confession to a non-crime. Their most fundamental Constitutional rights are being knowingly and blatantly denied in order to satisfy the appetites of the power hungry chomping at the bit. Its an ugly sight, but don't turn your heads. If you ignore this absurdity, soon it will be your heads on the chopping block.

Publius

IF WE DON'T STOP THEM NOW, THE POWER HUNGRY WILL KEEP ON EATING!

We got more information from our residents than we did from the Residence Life office. We didn't know what was going on. We had 270 other residents who wanted to know what was going on, and we couldn't tell them anything.

Although the poster battle occurred over a two-day period, Charles Graham and Mark Dally had had enough of it, and they filed for an injunction to stop Residence Life from barring their free speech. Charles indicated,

If we had not been supported by so many fellow residents, who just stopped by Mark's and my room, asking for more posters, and telling us how Resident Staff was clamping down on their hall, we might have quit, but they spurred us to fight for our rights. Freedom of speech would become the mechanism by which we would fight for our self-governance.

Mark commented, "We followed all the bureaucratic niceties and were rebuffed at every step; we showed all due diligence."

On November 4, 1987, Mark Dally and Charles Graham filed suit against Laura McMahan and Betty Dickinson, as representatives of Residence Life, in order to stop the removal of their protest posters, claiming this action violated their First Amendment rights of free speech. Laura recalled,

I read it in the newspaper, having just returned from my honeymoon. First, I had to figure out what happened. I was shocked, because I was completely unaware of the postering incident and, most certainly, the Office of Residence Life decision that these posters should be removed. I later learned that these posters were first posted on or about Saturday, October 24. On Monday, October 26, Dean Dickinson was asked by Charles Graham whether any posters should be removed from the public posting areas in the

> *residence houses. Dean Dickinson responded that the only posters which should be removed were the ones advocating violation of the University's security system. Because of questions which arose from the College students concerning whether Dean Dickinson was correct in this position, she informed the Resident Staff on or about Tuesday, October 27, to allow all posters to remain, regardless of their content.*

Reaction to the injunction from the Residence Life office was swift. Contact was made with the University General Counsel, who began to prepare for the university's defense. Focus on the College itself and the residents was diverted. Laura explained,

> *We were caught up in what we needed to do to respond to the lawsuit versus how we should respond to the day-to-day activities going on in the College. As soon as it became a legal issue, we were required to let the attorneys talk for us. The one thing I did do was to call and talk through the issue with the Resident Staff in Forman College and to write a letter to all Resident Staff telling them not to touch the posters.*

Even though the court case itself became a very specific battle of Charles Graham and Mark Dally against Laura McMahan and Betty Dickinson, the publicity was hard on the Resident Staff members. Helen Weber remembered,

> *I didn't get upset when it was my name in the paper, but when it became my staff who were being dragged through the mud, I got angry. . . . I did damage control with a totally demoralized staff. When the first round of mud was slung, I went around and rounded up all the staff; we went to MacDonald's and got breakfast (it was midnight), and we went to a playground where we could see Forman College. . . . Another time I kidnapped them all for a scavenger hunt*

through one of the academic buildings with Chinese food hidden as the treasure.

The College and the Residence Life office otherwise did not seem involved. Very few residents of the College showed up for the trial; some of the Resident Staff members were subpoenaed, but the trial otherwise was an issue for a very small group of people. Laura reflected, "To us, it looked as if the whole thing was settling down and that the College had become peaceful, once the fray was removed to the courtroom." On November 13, depositions were taken from the plaintiffs and the defendants concerning all the incidents that preceded the action. The court case received significant press coverage from the student press and regional newspapers. In February, the court decided in favor of the plaintiffs, Charles and Mark. The press presented mixed opinions but seemed to support the decision. The Resident Staff was barred from removing any posters, a practice that they had stopped before the case was filed.

The residents of Forman College, especially leaders of the press movement, thought they had a triumphant success. They soon realized that they were wrong.

From the Resident Staff perspective, University security policies such as the rules against door propping had to be enforced consistently. The judiciary charges proceeded after the court case. Lynn Chamber, Residence Life's judiciary representative, had talked with the University General Counsel and collected the depositions to use as evidence in the judiciary proceedings against both Charles and other named residents. Laura said of the judiciary trials, "It was the principle of the issue—security of our students—so we stuck with it for consistency's sake." As the judiciary trials proceeded, the Office of Residence Life tried to turn its attention back to the running of the other residential areas, but the tug-of-war between residents of the College and the Resident Staff continued.

Charles Graham recalled,

> *Within a week of the trial, residents, including myself, were being brought up on judiciary charges brought by the Hall Director, Helen Weber. Previously, she had no proof of who was propping doors open, but she obtained Mark's and my statements about the act of door propping, which were given in good faith at the Federal Court deposition. She obtained a copy of the depositions we had made in Federal Court from the University General Counsel. In these depositions I mentioned myself and a few other residents in reference to how we would prop a door open without damaging property. Never did I believe I was setting my friends and myself up to be prosecuted within the University by my sworn testimony in Federal Court. We had no idea that there would be a connection between this Civil case and our University judiciary case until copies of our sworn depositions were brought into the judiciary trial. This was the insidious behavior that sealed the hatred between residents and their Resident Staff wardens in the College.*

Ultimately, the judiciary system handed out several sanctions and threw two residents, referenced in the depositions, out of Forman College. The furor rose throughout the year, and the postering even moved into the freshman residence halls.

Questions before further reading:
- *Should legal depositions be used in University judicial proceedings?*
- *What role should students have in determining University policy?*
- *How do you supervise an area when you are receiving conflicting information?*

PART C - THE FINAL CHAPTER

Residents who thought they had won the battle ultimately felt that they had lost the war. Mark Dally reflected on the process, saying:

> *They never appeared to care what we thought; that is why we reacted so strongly. I think it all could have been resolved at that formal public forum, with a "big hug" and their indicating that they were listening, but they had to be right, so we saw no recourse. We needed to make them listen. To this day, we do not know why Resident Staff took this so seriously or why they were harassing us so much. We just figured that after the court case Laura McMahan and Betty Dickinson told Resident Staff to find violators and prosecute us.*

The Resident Staff in Forman College had thoughts of their own. Helen Weber remembered,

> *We were often told, "it's not you it's the Residence Life office"; the students were so angry. Nonetheless, we were caught in the crossfire. Just as they did not see us as the real enemy, we did not feel truly connected to Resident Staff. I needed more support, but I did not know how to ask. I had to enforce a policy, and my superiors did not seem to understand the position that put me in. Given the circumstances, I think we did a pretty good job; I hope all my staff knows how proud of them I am. It was a rough time, and yet we stayed very strong as a solitary unit.*

Finally, the administrators and the student Resident Staff co-chairs responsible for supervising and training the resident staff members and for providing a safe and educational living environment for students held their own point of view. Laura McMahan remembers,

The Office of Residence Life was stirred up by the tug-of-war occurring between residents of the College and the Resident Staff. The activities were somewhat perplexing to me. I believed the Resident Staff had been carefully counseled about how to handle the issues during the summer Executive Committee retreat and weekly meetings since the opening of school. We asked Resident Staff to talk with the residents and let them know that their actions could be jeopardizing the safety of other students. We told Resident Staff that they should try and work through these issues as a part of the community. With this constant guidance from the outset, the explosive activity of door propping was unfortunate. However, it was shocking when it led to charges of infringements of First Amendment rights and subpoenas from students.

We can learn several lessons that, if implemented, might have helped alleviate some of the autonomy versus centralization tension during the transition to the new security policy. It seems that expectations could have been managed differently. While the College students' governance rights were extensive, perhaps more attention should have been devoted upfront to establishing the context in which those rights would be exercised. Much of the tension surrounding the autonomy issue stemmed from the residents' feeling that they were not being listened to or heard. Earlier and more frequent communication regarding the rationale and genesis of the new security policy, as well as an explanation of the relationship and interaction between a University-wide security policy and students' right to self-governance, could have gone a long way towards dissipating some of the frustration before it turned destructive. Most importantly, supervision of our colleagues, students, and peers requires constant attention. The difficulty of balancing change, communication, and delegation of power is challenging enough in a routine situation. When the stress of an emotionally draining, politically volatile situation is added, this balance becomes the most critical element of all.

Given the occurrence of the rape and other security concerns, the change in policy was justified; however, its implementation could have been much more effective. One unresolved, critical issue for residents was the installation of security telephones outside every access door. It was not possible to have all of the security telephones installed before school started, so students were forced to resort to knocking and waiting for someone to admit them. Once the telephones were installed, all was not bliss, but there was a marked decline in the students' frustration level. Looking back, it is regrettable that more lead time had not been calculated ensuring that the telephones were ready when the students first arrived.

Although an undergraduate class memory usually does not extend beyond four years, remnants of the hard feelings between Residence Life officials and residents of the College have lasted ten years. No one really knows why the tension still exists. It tends to emerge in more subtle ways, but it is alive and well in the residents of this vibrant community. It may merely reflect the success of the ideals under which the College was founded.

Final questions about the case:
- *Why might the tension still exist?*
- *Should this tension be eliminated?*
- *What further action, if any, should be taken?*

Reflecting on Ethics Methods and the Case
Since we present this case as a tool for exploring various approaches to ethics, take some time to work through the following questions before moving on to the next chapter. Clearly, there are no right or wrong answers to these questions; they are designed to elicit your initial reactions to the case before working through different ethics approaches to it.

1. *Withholding any judgments about what occurred and about the individuals involved, what strikes you about "Do Your Part"?*

   Which parts of the case do you find the most compelling, and which were less interesting? What parts of the narrative make this a "case"? For example, do the legal aspects of the case or the relationships between the players interest you more? Often our initial reactions to a situation tell us what are the most important aspect to us. Although every aspect may have some interest, which captures your attention? This is an intuitive question that puts us on the path to, not the end of the road to further exploration.

2. *What values are reflected in your initial reactions to the case?*

   Do the policy issues in the case appeal to you because they offer a standard for consistency, or do virtues of the administrators catch your attention because you value your profession as a vehicle for personal growth? Do you respect the values of the students who defend their right to free speech, or are you more concerned that these students were willing to jeopardize the safety of other students? Do you recognize yourself in any of these characters?

3. *How do your values shape potential responses to this case?*

   If you were in the position of Laura McMahan, what would your response be to the students? Try to outline in detail which of your responses are virtue-based, rule-based, or consequence-based. For example, if you would have honored the students' demands for a different security policy, would your justification have been your desire for a peaceful resolution (favoring consequences) or maybe a sense that student self-governance is inviolable (favoring rules)? If you agree with Laura's action, do you value her courage and sense of justice (favoring virtues)? Putting yourself in the position of Laura McMahan or the hall director may reveal some aspects of the case that are not apparent from the narrative.

4. *Make a list of every possible point of tension in "Do Your Part."*
For each point, is tension created by the interactions among the players, the role of the rules or policies, a particular person's character, or the way that the conflict is addressed? Where are the normal points of tension and the more extreme conflicts? If two people have different working styles that may cause some disagreement, what makes this into a "case"? Which pressure points create the most questions in your mind? What are the internal conflicts for individual players, and what are the interpersonal tensions?

CHAPTER THREE

A Principles-Based Approach to Ethics

Scattered throughout "Do Your Part" are examples of various rules and principles that shape the actions and guide the moral decision-making of the participants. The Residence Life program had rules about not endangering other students by propping doors. The students in Forman College operated under the principles of self-governance. The students who sued various members of the Residence Life program invoked constitutional rules protecting the First Amendment right to freedom of speech. When considering different kinds of rules and principles, it is important to recognize that not all practical and legal rules are moral, only those that relate to how we interact with others and to self-directed actions. Although it is illegal in Virginia to walk on the lawn of the governor's mansion, this action is not immoral but, rather, nonmoral—not pertaining to morality. Similarly, Residence Life's rules about turning in keys at a certain time represent practical concerns rather than moral ones. Sometimes there is a stricter correlation between practical, legal, and moral rules, as with laws prohibiting murder, but caution should be used when assessing the morality of different kinds of rules.

Rules and principles provide norms for the acceptability of particular actions. A principles-based approach to ethics concentrates on the morality of actions, although concerns about agents and consequences are not entirely ignored. The injunction against Laura McMahan and Betty Dickinson in "Do

Your Part" demonstrates the consequences of breaking a rule that protects the freedom of speech for groups and individuals. Even this rule, however, has exceptions based on consequences. For example, one may not yell "Fire!" in a crowded movie theater and such exceptions suggest the complexity involved in assessing a system of morality based on rules and principles.

Principles-based approaches to morality face two fundamental questions: *What are principles?* and *Where do we get them?* To answer the first question, we will consider a principle as something that we can act on to guide us, or which we can breach (R. M. Hare, 1972). Principles, thus, can be said to morally prescribe actions. Because moral principles have the prescriptive force to shape our actions, the various sources of these principles deserve consideration. In addition to disagreements about the content of the rules, part of the difficulty in "Do Your Part" derives from discord about who in the institution has authority to impose rules on the students.

Another issue in this case depends on whether we consider rules to be unbreakable or whether we think they have exceptions. For example, if there are some instances when it would be acceptable to limit the speech of a group, how do we justify infringing upon the freedom-of-speech rule? The Resident Staff administrators were operating under another rule: to protect the safety of students when a risk is perceived. Given the conflict between the free speech rules and safety rules, we also have to address problems that arise when rules conflict with one another. *How do we decide which, if any, rule should be broken? How do we determine the consequences of such a breach?* In order to see the rules as part of a larger system of morality, we need to question the underlying values that inform them, to see if they could be expressed in other ways.

In this chapter, we analyze "Do Your Part" and other cases with the tools of a principles-based approach to ethics. Because such approaches operate most effectively as tools for conflict resolution, we draw close attention to the crisis points of the case. As we expressed in the introduction, however, we do not believe that this emphasis on crises adequately captures the complex moral issues involved in "Do Your Part." At the end of the chapter, we will reflect more deeply on the role of this approach in our moral lives given its appropriateness for resolving crises. In drawing on Tom L. Beauchamp and James F. Childress' (1994) work in this chapter, we will follow the tradition of using the term *principlism* to refer to their principles-based approach to ethics, even though the term was originally coined by critics of their project (Clouser & Gert, 1990).

We begin by briefly examining the principles Beauchamp and Childress delineate but focus on their *method* rather then the application of the principles to bioethics. Issues of autonomy in medicine will be very different from issues in student affairs, but by understanding their approach to ethics we can incorporate the components that are relevant to student affairs and lay aside components that do not seem as useful. Separating their approach to ethics from the four principles they discuss is crucial to understanding that the *method* of their principles-based approach is not invariably connected to its *substance*. Try to determine if this approach, which holds moral principles at its center, resonates with your own conception of morality. While reading this chapter, begin to answer some of the questions presented in the introduction, particularly the third question: *What role do principles or rules play in your life?*

BEAUCHAMP AND CHILDRESS' FOUR PRINCIPLES: *RESPECT FOR AUTONOMY, BENEFICENCE, NON-MALEFICENCE, AND JUSTICE*

In one way or another, all four principles presented by Beauchamp and Childress—*respect for autonomy, beneficence, non-maleficence,* and *justice*—are directly at issue in "Do Your Part." The brief sketch provided of the content of the four principles, as they are described in this and other texts on ethics, is meant to challenge you to question whether these principles make sense for your approach to ethics and, if they do not, to explore other kinds of principles that could operate in their place. For example, second-tier principles discussed by Beauchamp and Childress include *veracity, fidelity, privacy*, and *confidentiality*. As you try to make these personal decisions, keep in mind the distinction between moral and non-moral principles. An example of a moral principle is *beneficence* or *benefit others*. An example of a non-moral principle is, *never mix your colors and whites when doing laundry*. Since the second principle has nothing to do with the way we treat other living beings, it is an example of a non-moral principle and is not a concern in this monograph. (This is not meant to denigrate the importance of non-moral principles, particularly when washing white socks and a red shirt.) Focus your attention on moral principles that guide the way you navigate through interactions with others and see if they fit the principles suggested by Beauchamp and Childress.

Beauchamp and Childress define personal *autonomy* as involving a "personal rule of the self that is free from both controlling interferences by others and from personal limitations that prevent meaningful choice, such as inadequate information" (p. 121). Essentially, autonomy involves two conditions: a) liberty or freedom from controlling influences, and b) agency or the capacity for intentional action. Although it was not called respect for autonomy, the principle played a large role in the early history of student affairs. While students often came to college expecting an increase in their right to personal freedom, many university administrators saw themselves as students' guardians and made decisions on their behalf. Students, however, wanted to be respected as individuals and fought hard for the abolition of *in loco parentis* policies (Hoekema, 1994). The history of student affairs has involved a conflict between the principle of respecting students' autonomy and the principle of *beneficence*, which "refers to a moral obligation to act for the benefit of others" (Beauchamp & Childress, 1994, p. 260). The administrators invoked the principle of beneficence in order to justify imposing rules that were supposed to promote the best interests of the students. Yet, even in this simple example many questions arise: *Are all eighteen-year-old students capable of self-determination? If not, who should decide this? What is in the best interests of the students? Is it in their interests to impose curfews or is this a restriction of freedom?* The use of philosophical terms like autonomy and beneficence to describe commonsense morality can be distracting, but we encourage you to consider whether such principles are helpful in your everyday lives as student affairs administrators.

The students in Forman College felt that resident staff members were violating their right to autonomy by making decisions about their living environment. On the other hand, Resident Staff members worried about potential threats to student safety that accompanied door propping. Laura McMahan might have described the relevant principle here as *non-maleficence*, or the obligation not to inflict evil or harm on others. This principle is closely related to beneficence, which includes the duty to prevent or remove harm as well as to promote good. The distinction between not harming and benefiting others often blurs. In "Do Your Part," none of the students intended to harm others, but non-maleficence also includes negligence, the failure to meet certain obligations (Beauchamp & Childress, 1994). Living in a community of trust carries many different responsibilities, including care for the safety of others. If the students knew that their door-propping activities endangered the well being of other students, then they violated the principle of non-maleficence. If the community agrees not to harm others and to protect others against harm, it is a short step to arguing for the obligation to benefit them (Beauchamp & Childress, 1994).

Yet another way to describe the role of principles in the case is to examine the principle of *justice*. One formulation of the principle is that equals should be treated equally, and unequals should be treated unequally. This statement can be traced to Aristotle and is a formulation of the principle of formal justice. *Formal* refers to the indeterminacy of the principle since it lacks any criteria for determining who counts as equals or how they ought to be treated

(Beauchamp & Childress, 1994). In contrast, *material* considerations specify particular principles about how to justly distribute particular resources. Some examples of material principles include: *to each person an equal share, to each person according to need,* and *to each person according to merit* (Beauchamp & Childress, 1994, p. 330). These principles offer some guidance for distributive justice, but many questions remain, such as *how do we assess need or merit?*

In "Do Your Part," the Resident Staff Executive Committee members based the 24-hour security policy on the principle of justice in that all students living in university housing were considered equals and thus all were subject to the same policies. The students in Forman College, however, were not equal to freshman students in many respects and argued vehemently that they were in fact "unequal." Many aspects of Forman College differed from the freshman residence halls. All freshmen were required to live in residence halls, whereas Forman College students had to apply for the opportunity to live there. The design of the residence halls differed. The Resident Staff had a different role in freshman areas than in Forman. Finally, the founding mission of Forman College varied from the freshman living areas. Deans McMahan and Dickinson argued that these differences were irrelevant to the decision at hand and that all students living in university housing were subject to the same security policy. Treating various student groups fairly is a major concern for student affairs administrators, but careful attention must be paid to the relevant properties of the specific situation.

This presentation of Beauchamp and Childress' four principles offers an indication of how they function when applied to a concrete case. Take some time to try to identify other ways that respect for autonomy, beneficence, non-maleficence, and justice reflect the values of various people in "Do Your Part." *If you were one of the administrators in the case, would any of these principles offer you guidance in this situation? If not, do the second level principles of veracity, fidelity, privacy, and confidentiality better reflect your approach to ethics? Is this approach in general helpful to student affairs?* This final question is very important to our exploration of ethical approaches, and we will consider it in the next section.

PRINCIPLISM AND STUDENT AFFAIRS

In her work on the four principles in student affairs, Karen Kitchener (1985) draws on Beauchamp and Childress' model to "help practitioners understand and define the choices they face" (p. 17). By presenting their work and that of several other ethicists, Kitchener "provides student affairs with a common language and a set of precepts that can be effectively applied to moral problems" (Canon, 1993, p. 331). Although her work in ethics does offer a way to move beyond understanding ethics as merely adhering to professional codes, Kitchener has been criticized by Upcraft and Poole (1991) for drawing too heavily on the biomedical model of ethics presented by Beauchamp and Childress and Paul Ramsey (who contributed the principle "be faithful" to Kitchener's model). Upcraft and Poole (1991) argue that biomedical models may be relevant to Kitchener's field, counseling, since it shares the practitioner-patient model with medicine, but that this approach is not helpful for other areas of student affairs. Although Upcraft and Poole (1991) contend that the values of the biomedical model are not universally applicable, they unfairly attribute to Kitchener many shortcomings that are inherent to principlism and not a result of importing the approach to student affairs.

Upcraft and Poole (1991) offer an example of the inappropriateness of this principles-based model when they refer to the "erroneous injection" of autonomy into campus debates over rights, such as free speech. They contend:

This shifts the focus from the condition of the actor, as a moral agent, to legal protections that pertain to all persons, regardless of their moral autonomy. In other words, autonomy relates to one's mental and intellectual ability to make a decision rather than to the removal of legal and physical constraints on certain behaviors. The First Amendment right to free speech does not begin to address the degree of moral autonomy possessed by the speaker. (p. 85)

Upcraft and Poole are correct to note that autonomy requires the ability to make free and informed decisions, but they are incorrect in separating the removal of barriers from the purview of autonomy. In addition to the condition of agency, liberty is the second condition of autonomy, and it requires that individuals be "free from controlling interferences by others" (see definition of *autonomy*, p. 52). Such controlling influences often appear in cases relating to the First Amendment, as is the case in "Do Your Part," where students' rights to free speech were interfered with when resident staff members took down posters. Despite the objections raised by Upcraft and Poole, we believe there is some merit to exploring the way autonomy and the other principles operate in student affairs.

In this section, we are more concerned with the method Beauchamp and Childress use to arrive at the four principles than with their substance. To begin the exploration of this method, it is helpful to ask, *What makes someone a principlist?* According to Childress (1994), "at the very least, to be a principlist one must view general moral norms as central . . . without necessarily denying other features that are central in other frameworks" (p. 73). These general moral norms can take the shape of principles or rules that are meant to serve as action guides, sometimes prohibiting or requiring specific actions. One of the students in "Do Your Part," Mark Dally, is an excellent example of someone who holds moral norms as central in ethics. This is not to say that Mark was unconcerned with virtues or relationships. Yet, clearly, he was very dedicated to preserving the rules about free speech and student self-governance, and he freely violated other rules that conflicted with them (i.e. the security rules). For Mark, these rules reflected some deeply held principles, perhaps even absolute principles, and any infringement was viewed as a serious moral harm. *Do you sympathize with his stance? Do moral rules and principles hold a central spot in your moral life?*

In discussing Mark's reaction to the situation in "Do Your Part," we referred to *rules* and *principles*. Often these terms are used interchangeably, but there is a theoretical distinction. Ethicists define principles as broad values, such as *respect for autonomy*. Rules flow from these general principles and detail more specific guidelines, such as *do not make decisions for competent adults*. Yet Beauchamp and Childress note,

> *We also operate with only a loose distinction between rules and principles. Both are normative generalizations that guide actions, but, as we analyze them, rules are more specific in content and restricted in scope than principles. Principles do not function as precise action guides that inform us in each circumstance how to act in the way more detailed rules do. Principles are general guides that leave considerable room for judgment in specific cases and that provide substantive guidance for the development of more detailed rules and policies. (p. 38)*

Both principles and rules inform the judgments of individuals. In "Do Your Part," the specific rule prohibiting restraint of free speech comes from the Constitution of the United States and reflects the broader principle that we call the *right to liberty*. This principle values the rights of individuals to be free from a number of intrusions by the government and thus includes many different rules, such as refraining from searching someone's property without a proportionally grave cause. Most people do not distinguish sharply between principles and rules in the course of everyday life, so we will draw attention to this difference only when it is important to our position.

THE FOUNDATIONS OF PRINCIPLISM: COMMON MORALITY

Building on the foundation of what a principlist is, the next question seems to be, *Where do principles come from?* Beauchamp and Childress present a liberal communitarian account of the foundations and functions of principles, balancing the rights of individuals with the recognition that moral activity usually occurs in communities. Accordingly, they hold that it is unrealistic and unhelpful to treat autonomous persons as if they function without communal support or are free from communal obligations and traditions. The students of Forman College seemed to have lost sight of their position within the community of OSU and merely focused on their rights, which derive from a liberal tradition. This liberal communitarian approach to ethics builds on common morality to delineate the four principles that prohibit and prescribe moral actions. The phrase *common morality* deserves some analysis since it is both simple and complex. At one level, we all have an intuitive understanding of common morality: intentionally killing innocent people is wrong; torturing children for fun is wrong. No matter what your religious or cultural background, certain precepts hold. Beauchamp and Childress refer to common morality as socially approved norms of human conduct, such as those captured by the phrase, *human rights*. Common morality is embodied within ordinary language insofar as it is propagated by common sense and tradition. Common morality existed before we were born, and as we develop we are instructed in its rules. In "Do Your Part," the common morality at Old State University takes the shape of a strong emphasis on community and student self-governance. These values existed before the students and administrators involved in "Do Your Part" arrived at OSU and continue long after the incidents described in the case.

Although common morality is a pervasive element of our cultural environment, its principles are not necessarily uncontroversial. Social and cultural biases are, for example, transmitted through common morality. This can be seen in the history of student affairs administration in the policy of *in loco parentis*. At its inception, many professionals concerned with student well-being saw themselves in the role of parents. This philosophy carried with it many paternalistic attitudes that justified university policies on the basis that they were "for the good of the students." "[C]ollege authorities stand *in loco parentis* concerning the physical and moral welfare and mental training of the pupils, and . . . may make any regulation for . . . .betterment of their pupils that a parent could for the same purpose" (*Gott v. Berea College*, 1913). Even though most (male) students were old enough to be drafted, universities continued to treat them like children when it came to issues like curfews. This common morality continued as part of the infrastructure of student affairs until the general questioning of authority of the 1960s influenced university campuses. Students challenged the attempts to treat them like children and demanded respect as adults. Eventually, the focus in students affairs shifted from *in loco parentis* to its present emphasis on "student development" (Barr & Upcraft, 1990).

Beauchamp and Childress (1994) claim that common morality does not preclude the possibility of reform and that changes often occur through the processes of interpreting, specifying, and balancing moral principles. Yet, in situations involving deep biases such as race or gender preferences, such processes do not begin to touch the problem of the underlying cultural fabric. Reforming prejudices based in common morality is not impossible, but it does require the presence of a voice within the system willing to challenge the status quo. When a group is disenfranchised because of the prevailing beliefs of the common morality, reform may seem impossible. Although Beauchamp and Childress emphasize the evolution of common morality, it is unclear who the agents of change are and how problems in common morality get called to the public's attention. With the demise of *in loco parentis* policies, the culture of the 1960s signaled a radical shift in our common morality at many different levels. The 1964 sit-in and demonstration at the University of California-Berkeley launched a nationwide challenge to university authority that affected the role of student affairs professionals on campuses for many years (Bloland, Stamatakos, & Rogers, 1994). The students effected a shift in the common morality by rejecting rules imposed on them by university administrators. This challenge to the authority of rules demonstrates the importance of understanding how we justify various rules, which is the topic of our next section.

JUSTIFYING THE USE OF PRINCIPLES

The Berkeley demonstrations and "Do Your Part" show that rules are only effective if people believe that the rules apply to their situation and that they have some authority to develop those rules. Thus, it is important to question how we see principles coming to bear in our moral lives. *Why do we follow certain principles and rules? Are they rooted in an ahistorical source and handed down to moral agents, or do they develop from years of experience?* One method of justifying rules is *deductive*, and this can take several forms. Kantian philosophers look to reason as the ground of moral rules, thus removing them from the contingencies of history. The primary characteristic of deductive justification of moral norms is a preexisting, ahistorical, theoretical system from which moral principles and rules are deduced. With the deductive approach to moral norms, moral judgment merely involves the application of a rule to a particular case. The guidance for decision-making in the case comes from the "top down," which is another way to characterize the deductive approach (Beauchamp & Childress, 1994). This approach to informing students of a college's or university's policies and standards of conduct is used at many institutions and was a major point of contention in "Do Your Part."

The opposite side of this top-down application of moral rules is an *inductive* justification for norms. In this model, rules percolate up from the concerns of the people who will be governed by them. Induction involves reasoning from the specifics of cases to more general conclusions about the circumstances. This mode of moral justification focuses on particular situations and judgments as part of a dynamic moral life and will be more fully explicated in Chapter Four. Inductivists "propose that certain kinds of cases and particular judgments about those cases can be relied upon as warrants for the acceptance of moral conclusions independently of either general norms or a historical tradition" (Beauchamp & Childress, 1994, p. 18). As moral agents, we have various life experiences, and we learn to generalize beyond the judgments required for specific instances to apply our knowledge to analogous cases. The Forman College students preferred this method of justifying the existence of rules because it firmly rooted moral decision-making in a cultural milieu that supported student self-governance. This cultural context shaped the students' interpretation of moral rules and how they should develop. In the past, the students had contributed to policy decisions regarding their living environment. Based upon their knowledge of the specifics of their situation, the Forman residents believed they should be allowed to participate in the decision about the security policy. This justification of moral norms builds in the strength of flexibility that comes with experience but can face the charge of relativism. *What role do standards of moral conduct play when they do not arise from particular contextual judgments?* Sometimes general standards, such as our beliefs about protecting human rights, provide guidance for moral actions that do not emerge within our specific situation. Deductivism suffers from a static and unengaged account of morality while inductivism lacks a defined role for general moral norms. Each system of justification provides an essential part of the moral life that is not as helpful or as rich on its own.

Between the extremes of top-down and bottom-up moral justification lies a middle ground. Beauchamp and Childress' principlism is a *coherentist* approach that strives to balance the contributions of deductivism and inductivism. This dialectical approach to justifying moral principles acknowledges that although some rules are passed down to us, we can still have input into their continued interpretation. The principle of respecting student self-governance at OSU clearly remained an important part of the moral landscape, but new safety considerations led to its limitation. Beauchamp and Childress emphasize that the coherentist approach is the most practical way to honor principles drawn from various traditions while also allowing a flexibility necessary for the adaptation of the principles to changing circumstances. They derive this process of "reflective equilibrium" from the work of John Rawls (1971). Identifying "considered judgments" as "judgments in which our moral capacities are most likely to be displayed without distortion," Rawls argues that general theories can be built from these moral assessments (p. 47). If the theory is consistent with the paradigm's "considered judgments," then the resulting action guides should yield coherent results (Rawls, 1971). If the action guides are incoherent, then the process of reflective equilibrium between considered judgments and moral theories is reinitiated. This equilibrium is a dynamic state that needs careful pruning and attention if it is to be involved in the maintainance of a coherent approach to morality (Beauchamp & Childress, 1994). By diligently attending to the process of reflective equilibrium, the pitfalls of a purely deductive or inductive approach to moral justification can be avoided.

Beauchamp and Childress view ethical systems as dynamic and adaptable. They believe that their approach offers some protection against prejudices because it relies on this constant testing of theory and practice. Common morality brings us many principles that must be challenged and either re-accepted or altered to meet our moral needs. This may sound relativistic, suggesting that we can cast out principles when they no longer meet our needs, but the procedure for doing this is actually far more complex. The sexual revolution in the United States is one example of how common morality shifted with social and political trends. We are by no means finished with our attempt to refine rules about permissible sexual conduct, and tragedies such as the AIDS epidemic have caused us to rethink alterations in common morality. Similarly, we are facing a new attitude toward alcohol abuse in the aftermath of a series of deaths at college campuses. The point of a dialectical approach for justifying moral rules is to bring the weight of past experiences to bear on the concerns of contemporary society in a living and dynamic way. Otherwise, purely deductive or inductive systems can lead respectively to purely static or purely relative moralities.

A WORD ABOUT THE STRENGTH OF MORAL NORMS, OR HOW EASY IS IT TO BREAK A PRINCIPLE?

One crucial element of any moral or legal system based on identified rules is the presence of sanctions that can be brought to bear when someone breaks the rules. In order to levy punishments for infringing upon a rule, we have to understand the stringency of the rules. For example, some institutions' systems relating to cheating are relatively relaxed and cheating is often ignored. Other schools have stricter rules and will expel students for cheating. To understand these differences, we explicate three basic ways to describe the bindingness or weight of moral rules: *absolute, prima facie*, and *relative*. With *absolute rules*, you are wrong if you break the rule under any condition. In "Do Your Part," some students saw the principle of self-governance as an absolute rule, so breaking it was wrong regardless of other considerations such as student safety. Similarly, the Resident Staff program policy on locking doors was absolute and any violation of this policy resulted in judiciary actions.

When two absolute rules conflict as these did, there is no way to reach a compromise. The major philosophical model reflecting absolutely binding rules is Immanuel Kant's (1785/1981) account of categorical imperatives. Kant grounds his ethics theory in pure reason and argues that humans should only legislate rules that are universally binding and should aim to treat other persons as ends and not only as means. Morality depends on laws expressed in the nature of the acts and the duties that follow from the laws: "Duty is the necessity of an action done out of respect for the law. . . . Only the law itself can be an object of respect and hence can be a command" (p. 13). This absolute adherence to rules and the obligations they entail can create moral situations that defy any attempts at compromise. Some of the students in Forman College, whether acting out of Kantian respect for rules or from the thrill of opposing authority, were unwilling to yield on the issue of their "right" to determine policies for their living environment. *What would your response be in the face of such unwavering adherence to a rule? Do you, at times, cling this tightly to rules or laws?*

In contrast to absolutely binding rules, *relative* rules are better described as rules of thumb or guidelines. When we think rules are relatively binding it is quite easy to justify breaking them. There are no sanctions or repercussions to breaking relatively binding rules, since such rules of thumb merely suggest what other people have found helpful in the past. If the current situation seems to indicate better outcomes if you break the rule, then there is little hesitancy to break it. Some institutions' guidelines for assigning roommates serve as examples of rules of thumb. When the Office of Residential Life attempts to pair freshmen in residence halls, the staff may have formulas that suggest matching students from different states when possible. They may follow this guideline as an artificial convention to help speed along their placement process. But, if two students request each other as roommates, there may be little reason to strictly enforce this rule of thumb since the request of the students fulfills the function of expediting placement. If the rule involved segregating smoking and non-smoking students, stricter standards for maintaining this rule would be required. It is good to abide by relatively binding rules because they have proven effective in the past, but it is very easy to break them.

The middle ground between these degrees of stringency is found in *prima facie* binding rules. Literally, *prima facie* means "on first impression," that is, we can assume that, barring extenuating circumstances, a relevant rule or principle should guide our actions. If respecting student self-governance is a rule we value, we should abide by it unless extremely compelling circumstances arise. Since *prima facie* moral rules are binding, they can prescribe actions, and any departure from these rules must be justified. Several processes for justifying overriding *prima facie* binding rules are addressed in the following section.

Let us examine briefly the function of the rule *do not lie* in the following disturbing case to get a sense of how these weighing factors function. A freshman woman comes to you and tells you that her father has been sexually abusing her when he visits her at school. You help her move to a safe location, and she does not tell her father where she is living. When he arrives to visit her, he calls and asks you if you know her new address. You know you will

	***Prima Facie* Rules**	**Absolute Rules**	**Relative Rules**
Your Response	"I'm sorry, I can't answer your question."	"Yes, I do."	"I'm sorry, I don't know where your daughter is."
Your Reasoning	The rule prohibiting lying is very important to you as a foundation for trusting relationships. Yet the daughter told you her story in confidence and you do not feel that you should break this trust. Balancing the prohibition against lying with your duty not to harm, you decide to break the rule but you take steps to minimize the degree to which you break it.	It is always wrong to break a rule. The rule was established for a reason and we cannot violate it merely to ensure good consequences. You can try to persuade the father to seek help, call and warn the daughter, or otherwise try to prevent the abuse, but you cannot lie. To do so would be immoral and you don't know for sure that the father will abuse his daughter this time.	When someone's physical, emotional, and psychological well being are at stake, the best thing to do is protect the daughter even if this means lying. The rule against lying is merely a guideline that can be discarded in the name of safety. An abusive father does not deserve to know his daughter's address so you don't think twice about breaking the rule.

be lying to him if you say, "No, I don't know where she is," but if he finds her the abuse will continue. How do you respond?

Understanding how you evaluate the weight of rules is an important part of developing a consistent philosophy as a student affairs professional. Many jobs in the profession involve a disciplinary component and often require mediation when students break rules and policies. *Do you always apply a rule consistently, or do you believe that there is some room for discretion in deciding when and how to sanction students for breaking rules?* A situation you might face is enforcing policies related to underage drinking. If you walk through a residential area and see students drinking whom you know to be underage, *do you always initiate judiciary proceedings, or do you sometimes look the other way?* We all must obey and enforce rules in our daily lives; honestly assessing how we view the role of rules in our lives can help us become fairer and more consistent administrators.

HOW CAN PRINCIPLES HELP US ADDRESS CONFLICTS, AND WHAT HAPPENS WHEN THE PRINCIPLES CONFLICT?

One way to relate the principles to a certain situation is by merely applying the principles to a particular case. For example, we could apply the principle of beneficence (benefit others) to "Do Your Part," but this only raises more questions. *What do we mean by benefit others? Is it helpful to protect student self-governance or to protect student safety in their dorms?* Mere application of the principle yields little guidance.

One approach to refining the connection between the principles and individual cases involves *specifying* the moral norms that suit the given situation. Specification of moral norms assumes that they are not absolute (or we could not refine them to meet our needs) or relative (or else we could just get rid of the rule in a conflict) but that they do in fact provide some guidance in the case. By making our moral rules more specific, we should be able to tighten them to the point that our course of action becomes obvious (Richardson, 1990). In specifying the rule that protects free speech, we may accept, *Do not violate the free speech of individuals or groups as long as their actions do not present a real or predictable threat to other people.* Many of the exceptions to the First Amendment fall into this class. As Justice Holmes noted in 1919, it is not permissible to shout "fire" in a crowded building (*Schenck v. United States*, 1919).

One problem with the model of specification is that some moral disagreements may remain after tightly restricting the rule. Perhaps the security rule could require locking the doors during times when threats could be posed to residents. In this case, the students of Forman College differed from the Resident Staff in their understanding of what poses a predictable threat: they believed that locking the doors at night was sufficient while the staff believed that a possible threat was present 24 hours a day. With specification, we also run the risk of changing the norm beyond all recognition; this alteration of the rule would defeat the purpose of *prima facie* binding rules as having some prescriptive power over our actions. If the rule stated *Lock all doors when you see a person with a gun at the door*, it would be too specific to be useful in more general circumstances.

Since Beauchamp and Childress' four principles are *prima facie* binding, there can be tension between them and much room for interpretation in particular cases. We are not as concerned with labeling the conflicts between these principles (*autonomy* versus *non-maleficence*, for example) as we are interested in trying to uncover what it means when such a conflict arises. If you have a hierarchy of principles, then the dominant principle will win out when the two principles clash. When working with *prima facie* principles that are not ranked, conflicts are bound to arise and may be difficult to resolve unless there is a way to decide what happens when two principles do conflict.

Although specifying how principles function in a case is a crucial part of this decision-making process, sometimes no amount of specifying principles can eliminate conflicts. When two or more principles come into conflict, an additional method for resolving this tension is needed. *Balancing* moral principles involves considering the different weights of the principles in the case at hand and determining which principle is stronger in the situation. Beauchamp and Childress advocate an integrated approach to using specification and balancing the role of principles in cases. They also suggest that specification of principles is more helpful for policy decisions and that balancing provides more assistance in individual cases. *What would this process look like in "Do Your Part"?* Consider the possible role for the principles "autonomy" (right of self-determination) and "beneficence" (protect others from harm) in the case. From the administration's perspective, benefiting the students involved protecting them from crime by enforcing a 24-hour security policy. Failure to lock the doors may have produced significant harm to the students (one rape is one rape too many). But if autonomy requires promoting student self-governance, then this case presents the administration with a conflict. *Should student safety or student self-governance prevail?* By specifying these principles we may be able to draw more detailed conclusions about beneficence and autonomy and thus allow the preservation of both principles. Maybe the administrators specify autonomy to mean the right of self-determination as long as the physical safety of the students is protected. We must consider whether this specification compromises the original intent of the principle of autonomy. The students certainly did not feel that a significant enough threat was presented to justify the infringement on their rights of self-legislation.

In this case, specification does not really help reach a resolution, so we must employ the techniques of balancing. Given the potential dangers associated with unlocked hall doors, the weight of the principle of beneficence seems to be more substantial in this case than the principle of self-determination. When weighing the protection of physical safety against the right of student self-governance, the balance shifts in favor of student safety. One charge levied against the process of balancing moral norms is that it seems relatively random; if the students were asked to balance these norms, they clearly would have asserted the primacy of autonomy over non-maleficence. Even though specification and balancing can help resolve some conflicts between principles, we are still left with a complicated moral situation in need of attention. In later chapters, we will explore different ethical approaches that can enlighten other areas of the moral life and perhaps offer other forms of guidance.

Since some situations may necessitate overriding a principle, Beauchamp and Childress (1994) offer the following guidance to minimize the moral harm of overriding a *prima facie* principle:

1. The objective of breaking the rule should have a realistic prospect of achievement;
2. No morally preferable alternative should be available;
3. The form of the infringement should be the least possible;
4. The agent should seek to minimize the effects of the infringement. (p. 34)

This system rests on the assumption that the four principles are *prima facie* binding and thus require reasons for overriding a principle. If they were relative rules, then we could break them with ease. The four-fold conditions for minimizing the harm of infringing on principles also indicates that the agent breaking a rule should feel uneasy about the infringement; this sense of guilt helps to ensure that breaking the principle will not become a regular practice. If infringing on a principle becomes a regular practice without any lingering remorse, then the process of reflective equilibrium that justifies the presence of moral norms should be engaged to analyze the value of the principle.

SOME CRITICISMS OF PRINCIPLISM

"Throughout the land, arising from the throngs of converts to bioethics awareness, there can be heard a mantra '. . . beneficence . . . autonomy . . . justice . . .'" (Clouser & Gert, 1990, p. 219). This sentence occurs at the beginning of a famous critique that provided principlism with what was meant to be a pejorative name. Clouser and Gert argue that Beauchamp and Childress' principlism lacks an overarching moral theory to guide and sustain it when the principles come into conflict. The absence of a unified moral theory leads to the vapid application of principles to moral situations and often unresolvable conflicts between them. Beauchamp and Childress have responded to these criticisms by acknowledging that principles do conflict but that it is impossible to know *a priori* how to resolve this conflict. Only careful interpretation, specification, and balancing of principles will determine which principle overrides others in particular circumstances. The principles are not so hard and fast that they can be applied mechanically to all situations, as Clouser and Gert suggest. While these critics claim that a unified moral theory would provide a single, clear, and comprehensive process for decision-making, this belief reduces principlism to the type of foundational account of morality that Beauchamp and Childress specifically avoided. We agree that greater attention ought to be paid to problems related to conflicting principles, but we find Clouser and Gert's faith in an overarching guide to resolving conflicts naïve. Richardson (1990) and DeGrazia (1992) have offered more productive responses to this challenge.

In addition to the misinterpretation of principlism that assumes a mechanistic application of principles to cases, a second misconstrual of principlism is that the approach does not allow responsiveness to the particular forces at work in a particular case. Those who favor case-based approaches to ethics, specifically casuistry, charge that principlism fails to give adequate attention to particular judgments because it favors more general moral judgments (Childress, 1994). Casuists oppose the "tyranny of principles" (Toulmin, 1981, p. 31) represented by the mechanistic application of general moral rules to cases, yet this is not the model of principlism presented by Beauchamp and Childress.

> *[I]t is not the inevitable tyranny of principles as such, but rather the tyranny of some conceptions of principles particularly 'eternal, invariable principles, the practical implications of which can be free of exceptions or qualifications' (Jonsen & Toulmin, 1988, p. 2). Such principles lead to problems, particularly deadlocks and fruitless standoffs. And yet, as we have seen, most principlist approaches . . .*

in contrast to popular debate, recognize few if any absolute principles. (Childress, 1994, p. 83)

Casuists claim that principlism does not value the particularities of a case, and they over-emphasize the potentially deductive aspects of a principles-based approach. Principles and case-based approaches are not incommensurable, however, except that when a stalemate occurs, the principlist may use a principle to help break the tie while a casuist may point to the particular circumstances and to paradigmatic cases. The scales may tip toward rules for a principlist and toward particular facts for the casuist, but both methods involve a process of reasoning that draws on past experience and is open to revision. Chapter Four will address casuistry in more detail and demonstrate other potential areas of communion with principlism.

One of the most basic assumptions shared by principlists and case-based ethicists is an emphasis on autonomous decision-makers. Both approaches involve rational agents deliberating about their responses to moral situations with little or no explicit attention paid to their communities. A communitarian critique of principlism rejects approaches that focus on the liberties of individuals. While communitarians significantly contribute to ethical discussions by emphasizing historical traditions and communal values, Beauchamp and Childress stress that a false dichotomy is created when autonomy is pitted against community. Ideally, we would consider an autonomous person to be a member of a community whose decisions reflect social ties. Student affairs professionals face the difficult task of trying, on a regular basis, to balance the interests of individuals with those of the community. Chapter Five addresses virtue ethics and presents a longitudinal account of ethics that is more amenable to a communitarian project. We will explore communitarianism in the context of a virtues-based approach to ethics and will address further the issues related to individuals and communities in higher education institutions.

The final criticism we present questions how relational elements affect action in particular situations. Many student affairs professionals feel that part of their role is to serve as a friend or nurturer for students. The ethical model that addresses the nurturing part of our moral behavior is referred to as an *ethic of care* and grows out of the work of Carol Gilligan (1993) and Nel Noddings (1984). Gilligan argues that the dominant models of moral development reflect the perspectives of males and thus mistakenly assume that all people rely on abstract principles in moral decision-making. By reintroducing a feminine approach to morality, Gilligan argues that some people, particularly women, tend to make decisions that protect the people and relationships about which they care (Gudorf, 1994). She characterizes this as the difference between the *justice* (by which she understands principle-based reasoning) and the *care* approaches to morality. In addition to giving a voice to the moral reasoning more commonly used by women, Gilligan attempts to elevate relational approaches to morality to the same level as (or above) the male reliance on abstract moral reasoning. Although neither is deemed right or wrong, the intent of feminist models is to correct for the historical overemphasis on rational, rules-based moral reasoning. Gudorf (1994) states that

> *The basic problem with the principlist model is not that it relies on abstract principles, not that its particular principles emanate from male experience of the normative, but that both the reliance on principle and these specific moral principles function to regulate and maintain an unjust social system oppressive to women and other marginalized groups. (p. 168)*

While the strength of the feminist approach is the reclaiming of a voice for care and the "feminine" in moral reasoning, charges of relativism, arbitrariness, and favoritism all plague relation-based approaches to ethics. Another problem with an ethic of care is the temptation to align justice-oriented approaches with males and care-oriented approaches with females. Most people employ both approaches in varying combinations throughout their lives, and insisting on a strict separation is overly reductive. Despite these problems, feminism challenges all professional fields to assess the models and traditions that we accept in light of the perpetuation of systemic oppression of women. Keeping in mind the feminist critique of principlism will enrich our study of the role for ethics in student affairs. Gilligan and others have since relaxed the strict gender separation described above, but her observations revealed many new paths upon which few people had tread.

REFERENCES

Barr, M. J., & Upcraft, M. L. (1990). Identifying challenges for the future in current practice. In M. J. Barr, M. L. Upcraft, and Associates (Eds.). *New futures for student affairs* (pp. 3-21). San Francisco: Jossey-Bass.

Beauchamp, T. L., & Childress, J. F. (1994). *Principles of biomedical ethics* (4th ed.). NY: Oxford University Press.

Bloland, P. A., Stamatakos, L. C., & Rogers, R. R. (1994). *Reform in student affairs: A critique of student development.* Greensboro, NC: ERIC Counseling and Student Services Clearinghouse.

Canon, H. J. (1993). Maintaining high ethical standards. In M. J. Barr & Associates (Eds.), *The handbook for student affairs administration* (pp. 327-339). San Francisco: Jossey-Bass.

Childress, J. F. (1994). Principles-oriented bioethics: An analysis and assessment from within. In E. R. DuBose, R. Hamel, & L. J. O'Connell (Eds.), *A matter of principles: Ferment in U.S. bioethics* (pp. 72-98). Valley Forge, PA: Trinity Press International.

Clouser, K. D., & Gert, B. (1990). A critique of principlism. *The Journal of Medicine and Philosophy, 15*, 219-236.

DeGrazia, D. (1992). Moving forward in bioethical theory: Theories, cases, and specified principlism. *The Journal of Medicine and Philosophy, 17*, 511-539.

Gilligan, C. (1993). *In a different voice: Psychological theory and women's development.* (Rev. ed.). Cambridge, MA: Harvard University Press.

Gott v. Berea College, 156 Ky. 376, 161 S.W. 204 (1913).

Gudorf, C. E. (1994). A feminist critique of biomedical principlism. In E. R. DuBose, R. Hamel, & L. J. O'Connell (Eds.), *A matter of principles: Ferment in U.S. bioethics* (164-81). Valley Forge, PA: Trinity Press International.

Hare, R. M. (1972). Principles. *Proceedings from Aristotelian society, 73*, 1-18.

Hoekema, D. A. (1994). *Campus rules and moral community: In place of* in loco parentis. Lanham, MD: Rowman & Littlefield.

Kant, I. (1981). *Grounding for the metaphysics of moral* (J.W. Ellington, Trans.). Indianapolis, IN: Hackett. (Original work published in 1785)

Kitchener, K. S. (1984). Intuition, critical evaluation and ethical principles: The foundation for ethical decisions in counseling psychology. *Counseling Psychologist, 12*(3), 43-55.

Kitchener, K. S. (1985). Ethical principles and ethical decision in student affairs. In H. J. & R. D. Brown (Eds.), *Ethical principles and ethical decision making in student affairs* (New Directions for Student Services, no. 30, pp. 17-29). San Francisco: Jossey-Bass.

Noddings, N. (1984). *Caring: A feminine approach to ethics and moral education.* Berkeley: University of California Press.

Ramsey, P. (1970). *The patient as person; explorations in medical ethics.* New Haven, CT: Yale University Press.

Rawls, J. (1971). *A theory of justice.* Cambridge, MA: Harvard University Press.

Richardson, H. S. (1990). Specifying norms as a way to resolve concrete ethical problems. *Philosophy and Public Affairs 19,* 279-310.

Schenck v. United States, 249 U.S. 47 (1919).

Toulmin, S. (1981). The tyranny of principles. *Hastings Center Report, 11,* 31-39.

Upcraft, M. L. & Poole, T. G. (1991). Ethical issues and administrative politics. In P. L. Moore (Ed.). *Managing the Political Dimension of Student Affairs* (New Directions for Student Services, no. 55, pp. 81-93). San Francisco: Jossey-Bass.

CHAPTER FOUR

Case-Based Approaches to Ethics

In many professions—i.e., student affairs, law, business, and medicine—cases provide a major source of information. When trying to demonstrate a particular point or resolve a problem, we commonly refer to a landmark case or precedent as a way of assessing the current situation. Not only do cases import a sense of reality into heavily theoretical discussions, but their nuances and complexities also serve to catch our attention more than most academic writing does. The complexities of particular situations engage our interest and often mirror the relevant issue. For example, upon learning that a student stole money from a roommate, your decision-making process about sanctions may be influenced by the clarity of details of the case presented to you. If you are merely told "this is a case of stealing and the student confessed to it," your reaction may differ from a situation where you learn about the student's motives, personal situation, and remorse for his actions. Although the first approach is tidier, the second better represents the importance of rich descriptions in moral reasoning. "Cases are useful in teaching precisely because of their particularity. To smooth out the unevenness and sheer off the rough edges of a case history is to defeat the purpose of teaching by the case method" (Carson, 1986, p. 36). Using richly detailed real cases with untidy presentations is an important pedagogical consideration for a case-based approach to ethics (Arras, 1991, p. 37).

Despite these advantages of the case-based method, we need a stronger justification for using cases in ethics than their ability to convey complex information and to engage us. Case-based approaches to ethics, particularly casuistry, will guide our exploration of how we justify and use this method of ethical reasoning (Jonsen & Toulmin, 1988). Casuistry is a term derived from Latin and "today the word might be defined as the method of analyzing and resolving instances of moral perplexity by interpreting general moral rules in light of particular instances" (Jonsen, 1995, p. 344). The distinguishing feature of this method is its reliance on the particularities or the circumstances of each case, in light of the historical record of similar cases. When faced with a moral conflict between competing values in a case (good consequences versus a moral rule, for example), a casuist claims that attention to the details of the case and paradigm cases will help the agent discern the proper course of action.

> *The casuist would begin by identifying particular features in the case rather than appealing to universal principles, utilitarian calculations, or rights. The casuist would then attempt to identify the relevant precedents and prior experiences with other cases, attempting to determine how similar and different this case is from experiences with other cases. (Beauchamp & Childress, 1994, p. 92)*

In light of this sketch of casuistry, *how would a casuistic analysis of "Do Your Part" differ from the principlist model? What are the similarities and differences between these methods? Where would each approach start its moral analysis?* When trying to determine which approach is most appealing, consider whether you first thought of a rule or of the circumstances when assessing the case. Before discussing the contributions of casuistry to moral reasoning, we will explore consequentialism, another case-based approach to ethics, and its approach to moral situations. While reading this chapter, consider also the role that you think consequences should play in moral reasoning. *Are they more or less important than the nature of acts and the rules that govern them? Would you feel comfortable violating a rule if the circumstances of the case dictated it? How would we justify this?*

JUSTIFYING CASE-BASED REASONING: AN INDUCTIVE APPROACH

Before studying consequentialism and casuistry, we need a basic understanding of the justification for case-based ethics. *What gives this method its moral teeth*? Case-based ethics grows out of a repudiation of the scientific model of morality, which applies the methods of scientific theory to ethics, presupposing the existence of an orderly, overarching theory containing universal principles that are merely applied to cases. In rejecting such a model, casuists draw on Aristotle, and although they may accept generalized moral principles, they believe that they are drawn from personal and social actions. "Ethics is not a demonstrative science, but a set of practices and types of judgment rooted in experience, wisdom, and prudence" (Beauchamp & Childress, 1994, p. 94). This process of reasoning from the case to more general principles is an example of the "bottom-up," or inductive, justification presented in Chapter Three. According to John Arras, a philosopher and bioethicist at the University of Virginia, a case-based approach to ethics "insists that our moral knowledge must develop incrementally through the analysis of concrete cases" (Arras, 1991, p. 31). When done properly, ethical analysis of a situation begins in concrete cases and not with moral principles or theories. "It's not as though one could or should first develop a pristine ethical theory planing above the world of moral particulars, and then, having put the finishing touches on the theory, point it in the direction of particular cases" (Arras, 1991, p. 32).

In "Do Your Part," Laura McMahan was faced with her duty to preserve a safe living environment in Forman College and her knowledge that enforcing this policy would bring about unpleasant consequences. In order to resolve this conflict, we can look at the circumstances of the case and see if they shed any light to guide Laura's actions. When considering the safety issues at Forman College, particularly the fact that leaving one door unlocked allows access to the whole facility through underground tunnels, it became clear to Laura that she could not allow the safety policy to be ignored. Even though she realized that this would cause unrest among the students, the circumstances of the case indicated that a significant safety threat could be posed if the doors to Forman College were not locked 24 hours a day. In another institution with different circumstances, however, the student affairs staff may have decided that it was more important to preserve the sense of student self-governance than to enforce the policy. Perhaps the buildings at another school have central reception areas through which any intruder would have to pass in order to infiltrate the building. At that school, the circumstances would not necessarily dictate enforcing a 24-hour security policy because other measures could ensure security. In contrast to the principles-based approach to ethics, the particularities of the case itself, and not moral norms, dictate the proper course of action. One type of case-based approaches to ethics appraises the circumstances of cases in light of the future consequences of actions. The next section will examine the features of the consequentialist approach to ethics.

CONSEQUENTIALISM

In order to determine the morally right thing to do in a particular case, consequentialists try to predict the outcomes of their actions based on the circumstances at hand. "Actions matter only insofar as they create consequences and agents are important only because they are able to act in ways that produce good consequences" (Wicks, Spielman, & Fletcher, 1995, p. 240). After predicting the outcomes of actions, consequentialists next consider how to evaluate the effects of these actions and who performs this evaluation. "The right act in any circumstances is the one that produces the best overall result, as determined from an impersonal perspective that gives equal weight to the interests of each affected party" (Beauchamp & Childress, 1994, p. 47). This approach requires a degree of omniscience, not only in predicting the future results of actions, but also in seeing and impartially evaluating their impact on each affected party.

Within this approach, we also must consider the standards for judging the results of actions. The most prominent one is the principle of utility. It may seem contradictory to have a principle justify the case-based approach of consequentialism, but it is important to remember that moral theories differ in their emphases on the various components of morality. All moral situations involve agents, acts, and circumstances. Utilitarianism is most concerned with maximizing good results in given circumstances, but a principle guides us to this goal. *What kinds of values would guide you if you were performing a consequentialist evaluation of an action?*

The principle of utility assesses moral acts by their ability to produce the greatest balance of good over evil (Frankena, 1973). Jeremy Bentham and John Stuart Mill advocate a hedonistic version of the principle of utility since pleasure and happiness are considered good, while pain and unhappiness are to be avoided. In his famous essay, "Utilitarianism," John Stuart Mill (1962) offers the following description of the principle of utility:

> *The creed which accepts as the foundation of morals, Utility, or the Greatest Happiness Principle, holds that actions are right in proportion as they tend to promote happiness, wrong as they tend to produce the reverse of happiness. . . . The happiness which forms the utilitarian standard of what is right in conduct is not the agent's own happiness but that of all concerned. (1962, pp. 257, 268)*

When considering our conduct in particular circumstances, we must ask, *what action will produce the greatest possible benefit with the least possible burden for all individuals affected by it?* The principle of utilitarianism is often stated as "do the greatest good for the greatest number" or "maximize benefits and minimize burdens." *Act* utilitarians believe that only the principle of utility should justify particular judgments; moral rules can offer some guidance but are expendable if they do not promote utility. If faced with a situation concerning lying to a student, an act utilitarian would merely consider the situation at hand and whether it maximizes utility. If lying promoted general happiness, then the act utilitarian would break the rule "do not lie." In contrast, *rule* utilitarians believe that following moral rules maximizes utility over the long term. The trust built into a community that follows the rule *do not lie* can bring great advantages. Routinely breaking a rule, even if it produces short-term benefits, can damage the fabric of the community. Thus, the rule utilitarian would follow the moral rule, as long as it is justified by utility, and would not view lying as justified (Beauchamp & Childress, 1994).

The utilitarian version of consequentialism is an approach to morality often invoked by student affairs administrators. So much of our time is spent trying to mediate situations where the good of the individual may conflict with the good of the community. The students in "Do Your Part" demanded the right to leave their doors open for their convenience, but this was potentially putting all members of the community at risk. In this case, overriding the interests of individual students to benefit the community at large was clearly problematic even though the reasoning behind the policy was sound. Given the indeterminacy of the definitions of utility, we must be very careful when relying on this approach to morality. Assessing future consequences of actions for values such as "happiness" or "benefit" is rife with subjectivity and some charge that this could lead to sanctioning immoral acts in the name of utility. *What if the administrators kicked all protesting students out of Forman College in order to protect the safety of the other students? Would this be justified? At a more extreme level, what if expelling a student from school protected the community from his inflammatory speech?* Given the potential dangers of consequentialism and the difficulties inherent in its subjective valuations, we turn to casuistry, another case-based approach to ethics. We believe this method will be familiar to student affairs professionals since it is similar to the legal model. Casuistry offers a more specific procedure for decision-making that includes a step of critical review following the moral decision. Prospective and retrospective accountability for moral decision-making should be encouraged in our personal and professional lives and those of our colleagues.

CASUISTRY

While consequentialism focuses on the future outcomes of actions in particular circumstances, casuistry looks to the past for moral guidance and seeks to place the current decisions in the pattern of this whole. Consequentialism's range of vision is narrowed to specific acts and their potential results, whereas casuistry is concerned with creating points of coherence between the present and the past. Consequences can be part of the moral calculation for a casuist, but they are not its focal point. In casuistry, an inductive justification for moral reasoning orients the locus of morality in the particularities of the case, and more general moral norms are formulated from paradigm cases. Looking to the past for paradigmatic cases guides the current process of moral decision-making. Moral rules percolate up from cases and can serve as guidelines when similar situations arise. These guidelines (or principles) can be generalized to cases with similar features but are not universally applicable because their content depends on the specific circumstances of the case (Jonsen & Toulmin, 1988). "Rather than serving as a justification for certain practices, principles within the new casuistry often merely seem to report in summary fashion what we have already decided" (Arras, 1991, p. 34). Even though guidelines emerge that shape our behavior, this does not mean they apply universally. The process of interpreting the guidelines is dynamic and allows for their revision in the event that future cases show that they are no longer applicable.

For example, in professional basketball, a guideline or rule of thumb is to not foul outside the three-point line. This guideline is not part of the top-down official basketball rules all players must follow, which are deductively justified. Rather, it is a shorthand way of communicating information from past experience which showed that fouling outside the three-point line is a waste of a foul because it gives the other team the chance to put more points on the board. Consider, however, a tight game with five seconds left and your team is up by three points. In these circumstances, it may be a good strategy to foul a ball handler outside the three-point line before he can shoot a three-pointer and tie the score. At worst, this sends the ball handler to the line for two free throws since it was not a shooting foul. Inductive reasoning created a rule of thumb which offers some guidance, but casuistry also requires skillful interpretation as to when a guideline may not apply.

The guidelines that emerge from paradigmatic cases are similar to precedents set in the common law model. In common law, decisions in individual cases set new societal standards by which relevantly similar cases are then judged. "Casuists see moral authority similarly: Social ethics develops from a social consensus formed around cases. This consensus is then extended to new cases by analogy to the past cases around which the consensus was formed" (Beauchamp & Childress, 1994, p. 95). In the legal system, the convention of *stare decisis* (to stand by that which was decided) highlights the value of precedents and indicates the care that should be taken when considering overriding a previous court's decision. General moral norms grow out of consensus about cases and can offer parameters of acceptable action, but they remain open to reformulation with due consideration. One problem with grounding an ethical approach on social consensus is that, lacking a "stable framework of general norms," it is difficult to prevent the perpetuation of social prejudices in the system (Beauchamp & Childress, 1994, p. 97). Social consensus sanctioned extremely racist acts throughout the first part of the twentieth century, and our system of common law was deficient in responding to bigotry. Common morality and consensus models fail to offer sufficient protection against the perpetuation of social injustice by those in power. Justifying moral acts based on past experiences can provide a more practical model for moral decision-making than "top-down" approaches, but the costs should be carefully considered.

HOW DO WE PERFORM A CASUISTIC ANALYSIS OF A SITUATION?

Someone working within a casuistic model will charge that principles-based ethics does not pay enough attention to the circumstances of individual cases. This focus on circumstances means that case-based ethicists will explore the unique features of "Do Your Part." Rather than drawing from general principles as the locus of moral deliberation, this case-based approach will examine the unique characteristics of OSU, Forman College, and the personalities of the people involved. Some questions relevant to this exploration may include the following: *Did the culture of OSU foster the students' discontent, or could this case have happened anywhere? Could the situation in "Do Your Part" develop in this way without this unique mix of students and administrators?*

After exploring such questions about the particular nature of the case, one of the greatest challenges present in "Do Your Part" is deciding what kind of case this resembles. *Should we classify this as a residence hall dispute, a challenge to university authority, a constitutional law issue, or a question regarding student safety?* Classifying the case involves identifying one or more paradigm cases with which to compare the current situation. These paradigm cases help locate points of moral certainty that act as footholds for orienting ourselves in the case at hand. The final aspect of a casuistic analysis is a critical review of the movement between new and old cases. Sometimes this process sheds light on old cases and helps us refine their position in our moral lexicon (Juengst, 1989). The rest of this section is devoted to the three components that we will use to assess some of the issues in "Do Your Part."

Step One: Describe the unique features of the case.

The first step in a casuistic approach to a situation is to determine the *structure* of the case. Cases relating to certain topics that arise in professional fields will include similar issues. For example, cases that fall under the broad category of "ethics in student affairs" include (among others) the following topics: a) relationships with supervisors; b) relationships with employees; and c) quality of service provided to students. Job descriptions, the mission of the division, and common sense all contribute to our knowledge of these invariant features. Each topic concerns certain elements that must be considered in every case. Whether we are faced with the case of a vice chancellor diverting funds to pay for personal expenses or a middle manager having difficulties with a group of students, all of these issues would apply because they are invariant features of this category. Once we understand the invariant features of the case, we examine the variant or particular features of the case at hand. "The particular circumstances of time, place, personal characteristics, various behaviors, and so on that are the details of any case are viewed in the light of these topics" (Jonsen, 1995, p. 349).

One issue raised in "Do Your Part" that should be discussed is Dean Dickinson's response to Helen Davis when Helen told her that the Forman College resident staff members were taking down posters. In assessing the Dean's response, we must consider the three topics suggested above. Dean Dickinson initially responded that it was Helen's, not the Residence Life Office's, decision to take down the posters. As a supervisor evaluating an employee, this response was technically correct, but it made Helen and her staff feel isolated in a difficult situation. After talking to her supervisor, Laura McMahan, Dean Dickinson regretted her response, apologized to Helen, and emphasized that Residence Life would support the staff in the conflict over propping the doors. Dean Dickinson's initial reaction to Helen affected the service that the Residence Life Office was supposed to provide to the students in Forman College. Although the Dean rectified her response, it exacerbated an already tense situation.

Evaluating the particular events related to this case in light of the topics listed above can help us figure out what kind of case is before us. This part of the process may be called *getting clear on the facts*, but it is important to recognize that information can be skewed by its source. When assessing a case, we should make every effort to talk with as many people as possible about the situation and to remain open to the possibility that there are alternative versions of the events. Distilling the information should reveal the major features of the case, and conflicting details may be attributed to the role the source of information played in the events. All of the circumstances related to the incident will shape our moral judgment, so it is particularly important that we have the least biased account of what actually happened in the case. Once we have accumulated enough information about the situation, we can then place "Do Your Part" into a context of similar cases (Jonsen, 1995, p. 349).

Step Two: Place the case into a context of similar cases.
Understanding the structure of the case in terms of its topics and circumstances allows us to proceed to the second level of analysis. Since the structure of a case involves invariant and variant structures, there is some latitude when it comes to deciding how to classify the case. We can categorize the case under various types of issues such as residence hall disputes, safety considerations, or student rejection of authority. This allows us to look at paradigm cases that relate to the one at hand.

> *This technique of lining up cases, rather than seeing them in isolation, is the essence of casuistical analysis. It is called by some authors the technique of paradigm analogy: The paradigm case is the case in which circumstances allow moral maxims and principles to be seen as unambiguously relevant to the resolution of the case; the analogies are those cases in which particular circumstances justify exceptions and qualifications of moral principles.* (Jonsen, 1995, p. 349)

In thinking through "Do Your Part," we might consider applying cases related to "campus security issues and the degree to which colleges are responsible for protecting students from their own actions and the acts of others" (Kaplin & Lee, 1997, p. 13). This string of cases, beginning with *Mullins v. Pine Manor College* (1983), provides a basis that allows student affairs professionals to analyze and dissect the actions in "Do Your Part." *Mullins* established the legal duty of a residential college to employ due care in providing campus security.

> *The threat of criminal acts of third party parties to resident students is self evident, and the college is the party which is in the position to take those steps necessary to ensure the safety of its students. No student has the ability to design and implement a security system, hire and supervise security guards, provide security at the entrance of dormitories, install proper locks, and establish a system of announcement for authorized visitors. . . . Thus, the college must take the responsibility on itself if anything is to be done at all. (p. 335)*

Another case that provides the opportunity for further analysis, *Miller v. State of New York* (1985), confirmed that "[a] special relationship existed between the student and her university, and the institution's failure to lock the outer doors of the dormitory was a breach of duty as well as a proximate cause of the rape" (Gibbs, 1992, p. 51). In each of these cases, it is an assumed fact that outdoor locks, at the very least, must be engaged.

This same type of scrutiny and analysis can be applied to cases based on experience rather than legal precedent. Placing a particular case on a spectrum of other cases involving similar issues allows us to see the similarities and differences between the cases, especially "those cases in which the moral principles and maxims appeared to lead to an unambiguous resolution" (Jonsen, 1995, p. 349). A critical part of this process involves examining a range of cases that vary in their degrees of certainty about the present issue. Comparing the current case to only one paradigm case is inadequate. Classification of the case is a critical step in this casuistic analysis, as it determines the other resources that will bear on our assessment.

The process of analogical reasoning is the heart of casuistry, both as its method for decision-making and as the locus of moral certainty. "A high degree of assurance, or moral certitude, pertains to the resolution of paradigm cases, while varying degrees of moral probability, or probabilism, attach to the resolution of analogous cases" (Jonsen, 1995, p. 349). Experience tells us that it is wrong for student affairs administrators to have sexual relations with students, but cases involving older students who do not have any formal relationship with the administrator are not so clear. Thus, harsh judgment may be due to a dean who forces a student to provide sexual favors in exchange for positive reviews at the end of an internship, but perhaps we can excuse certain other relationships between administrators and students. We can generalize rules emanating from paradigm cases to other cases with similar characteristics, but the rules always require interpretation. This is very different from the approach of someone who believes in absolutely binding principles; such an individual would maintain that all acts involving sexual relations with students are immoral and cannot be justified by the circumstances. Inspector Javert, in Victor Hugo's classic epic *Les Miserables* (1862/1997), demonstrates this absolutist position by showing no mercy for Jean Valjean, who stole a loaf of bread to feed his starving family. Javert was only concerned with the fact that Valjean had broken the law. A casuist interpreting the case of Jean Valjean would note that he had violated a moral maxim, but might not be inclined to sanction Valjean given the relative insignificance of the crime. Avoiding the proclivity to make humans slaves to the law or principles is one of the major strengths of the casuistic model.

In "Do Your Part," Charles Graham operates as a casuist in his reactions to the security policy. He examined the method used to develop the new security policy and compared it to other cases of policy implementation in Forman

College. Charles was not concerned with questions about breaking rules or principles but with the fact that the implementation of this policy differed from that of other policies in his residential area. This comparison revealed that the students in Forman College had been given more input in previous policy discussions about their facility, so Charles protested the imposition of the policy and rallied the other students to do the same. He did not decide to oppose the policy because he felt that the principle of self-governance was violated; rather, he looked around at other cases and saw that this situation was treated differently. Of course, a different student looking at this situation might have thought that students were given entirely too much input into policies related to their safety. In looking back at precedent cases, such a student might wonder if they were handled properly. This retrospective evaluation of the process of analogical reasoning is the third component of casuistry.

Step Three: Evaluate the movement between different cases.
The third and last component of a casuistic analysis involves the movement created by reasoning between paradigmatic and analogous cases (Jonsen, 1991b). Traditionally, "casuists' thinking moved from the clear and obvious cases toward the more problematic ones. They had a base, the manifest relevance of a strong principle to a certain case, and moved away from that base by the addition of complicating circumstances" (Jonsen, 1986, p. 71). Moving between different cases reveals various features that may remain masked without the benefit of such comparisons. The motion may entail shifting moral judgments. We may say that an action is wrong in relation to a paradigm case, but in the analogous case, the same action could be justified by the particular features of the case. This movement also contributes to a self-corrective process that shields casuistry from charges of relativism. Re-examining accepted precedents in light of new information ensures that the paradigms do not become stale and irrelevant to current cases (Juengst, 1989). Casuistry continually expands the range of cases whose moral implications

we know with some semblance of certainty, providing a mechanism for evaluating previous conclusions about whole series of cases. While *stare decisis* protects precedents from capricious attempts to discard them, reconsideration and revision are the lifeblood of common law and common morality. Indeed "the moral certainty with which we invest our paradigms, in other words, depends less on the acuity of our moral vision than on the degree to which they have been tempered in the crucible of changing circumstances, increasing knowledge, and accumulated human experience" (Juengst, 1989, p. 26).

With a sound understanding of the structure of the case and its classification as a foundation, a moral agent who has the practical wisdom (*phronesis*) to skillfully move back and forth between cases can resolve the conflict. In order to achieve a richer case assessment, Carson (1986) recommends combining reflective modes of interpretation that try to answer questions about meaning with more critical modes aimed at analyzing the case. The resolution of the case thus depends on moral wisdom or "the perception of an experienced and prudent person that, in these circumstances and in light of these maxims, this is the best possible moral course" (Jonsen, 1995, p. 349). One develops this skilled reasoning by reflecting critically on human experience and the human condition; clearly, this method can run into trouble if inexperienced agents are involved. This is not to suggest that only enlightened agents can practice the art of casuistic reasoning, but we want to emphasize the importance of common sense and self-reflection.

> [C]asuistry, for all its usefulness as a method, is nothing more (and nothing less) than 'an engine of thought' that must receive direction from values, concepts and theories outside itself. Given the importance such 'external' sources of moral direction must play even in the most case-bound approaches, teachers and students need to be self-conscious about which traditions and theories are in effect driving their casuistical interpretations. This means that they need to devote time and energy to studying and criticizing the values, concepts

and rank-orderings implicitly or explicitly conveyed by the various traditions and theories from which they derive their overall directions and tools of moral analysis. (Arras, 1991, p. 41)

Component	Questions
Structure	*Invariant features:* What ethical questions arise from the case? What are the topics of the field and how do they relate to this question? *Variant features:* Who are the people involved and what are their characteristics? ■ Where did this situation take place? ■ What are the details of the actions? ■ Was anyone harmed or helped? ■ Did anyone break the law? ■ What kind of institution was involved? ■ Does religious affiliation play a role? ■ What are other contextual considerations?
Classification	What are other cases that remind you of this one? ■ In this realm of cases, what is a paradigm case where the moral judgment is certain? ■ How does the case at hand compare to the paradigm case? ■ Are there other ways to classify this case? ■ Would this change your actions in the case?
Movement	What do I learn when I move back and forth comparing this case to others? ■ Does this movement confuse the situation or help clarify the issues? ■ Am I skillfully navigating between the principles in the paradigm cases and my case?

THE ROLE OF MORAL PRINCIPLES IN CASUISTRY

For a casuist, moral principles emerge from cases and summarize our experiences in a series of related cases: "the meaning and scope of moral principles is determined contextually through the interpretation of factual situation in relation to paradigm cases" (Arras, 1991, p. 37). Jonsen (1988) notes that casuistry is not inimical to principles, but neither is it merely situational or contextual. While a case-based approach to ethics gives higher priority to circumstances, it also sees that principles are relevant to cases in varying degrees. It is only the inflexible interpretation of principles that leads to the criticism of principles as tyrannical (Toulmin, 1981). More moderate casuists recognize that in some cases, the relevant guideline should be applied unequivocally, whereas other situations call for a modification of the rule (Jonsen, 1995). This explicit acknowledgment of the role for general moral norms in casuistry deflects some criticisms about its tendency toward relativism.

Yet, this does not answer all criticisms about the weak role for moral norms in some casuistic approaches. Some defenders of principlism "contend that it is better first to recognize that general moral considerations, which can be called principles, function broadly in our judgments and then to examine them directly for their adequacy rather than allow them to enter covertly" (Childress, 1994, p. 84). Since casuistry does not place a strong emphasis on moral norms, even though they clearly perform a needed role, and favors moral guidance that emerges from cases, this may be one point where principlists and casuists must "agree to disagree." Jonsen explains that casuistry seldom relies on one principle to justify a moral situation:

Justification of any particular moral claim rarely comes from a single principle, as many theories would like, but usually from the convergence of many considerations, each partially persuasive but together convincing with plausible probability;" after all, "the weight of principles comes less from themselves than from the facts they carry in any particular case. (Jonsen, 1991a, p. 15)

The interplay between the case and the moral maxims creates a dynamic tension that is reminiscent of Rawls' process of reflective equilibrium discussed in Chapter Three. While "casuistry is not simply applied ethical theory . . . it is not simply immersion in the factual circumstances of cases, which would reduce it to situationism" (Jonsen, 1995, p. 349). This dialectic between general principles and cases was also seen in Beauchamp and Childress' principles-based approach to ethics; the main difference lies in the emphasis given to these two entities. While Beauchamp and Childress favor general principles in moral judgment, Jonsen, Toulmin, Arras, and other casuists prefer knowledge drawn from concrete cases. This distinction should not be downplayed since it shapes the way we evaluate moral cases, but we believe that it is a mistake to argue that these are two completely distinct theories with little room for dialogue. Rather, we advocate examining the similarities between principles- and case-based ethics because they share a crisis-oriented approach to morality. Contrast this with a feminist approach to ethics that looks toward care and responsibility in personal relationships as the proper locus of moral concern. A feminist account of morality thinks that both principlism and casuistry wrongly emphasize relatively individualistic, rationalistic accounts of how we should treat other people. Similarly, someone from a non-Western culture could look at the politics in the United States and see rather slight differences between Democrats and Republicans, given the presence of ultra-liberal or ultra-conservative political parties around the world. Variances between casuists and principlists could better be described as a family quarrel than as entirely different approaches to morality.

CRITICISMS OF CASUISTRY

One of the most critical objections to secular casuistry is that it has no real moral authority. Historically, casuistry developed within the Roman Catholic Church and drew on the Church's hierarchy of moral values as a source of authority. Similarly, legal casuistry relies on common law that is based in the authority of the courts. By contrast, "moral authority, in the secular world, is vested, primarily, in the moral agent and not in the agencies of society" (Wildes, 1993, p. 35). Since we lack a sound foundation to yield determinate answers to moral problems, Arras notes

> *Indeed, anyone familiar with Alasdair MacIntyre's (1981) disturbing diagnosis of our contemporary moral culture might well tend to greet the casuists' announcement of moral consensus with a good deal of skepticism. According to MacIntyre, our moral*

culture is in a grave state of disorder: lacking any comprehensive and coherent understanding of morality and human nature, we subsist on shattered shards and remnants of past moral frameworks. (Arras, 1991, p. 42)

Given the variety of sources for moral authority, drawing on past experiences for guidance with current cases is bound to lead to conflicting decisions. "Contrary to the assurances of Jonsen and Toulmin, the new casuistry is an unlikely instrument for generating consensus in a moral world fractured by conflicting values and intuitions" (Arras, 1991, p. 43). In response, Jonsen and Toulmin (1988) disagree with this characterization of a "shared world view" backing casuistry. On the contrary, they believe that historic casuistry was a response to a fragmented world view within the Catholic Church that had fueled moral doubts. Casuistry attempted to restore some stability to the process of moral reasoning (Juengst, 1989). Casuistry is not the only ethical approach that lacks a common worldview; theory-based approaches to ethics, such as John Rawls' account of justice, also fail to provide uncontroversial sources of moral authority. Arras concludes, "Neither theory nor casuistry is a guarantor of consensus" (Arras, 1991, p. 44). Ultimately, it appears that Jonsen and Toulmin's casuistry is vested in the moral agent and not in an "agency of society." Arguments for a common morality as the base may help firm up the ground of casuistry, but the process remains firmly rooted in the individual.

Even though casuistry moves away from universal principles in favor of moral reasoning grounded in circumstances, feminists argue that it is still too individualistic and rationalistic. Arras makes a similar point: " . . . it seems that the casuists' method of reasoning by analogy only promises to exacerbate the individualism and reductionism already characteristic of much bioethical scholarship" (1991, p. 46). The casuist process of moral deliberation tends to narrow our vision to relevant cases and does not encourage broader, imaginative questions about the situation. Relationships merely provide another contextual consideration without any normative weight in the process. Some feminists believe that the relationship between two people and their care for each other should figure more prominently in a moral evaluation than should the precedents set by old cases. These precedents contain many social prejudices that have oppressed women over the years and have distorted values that are important to women. This criticism of casuistry is critical to understanding how deeply entrenched many of our assumptions are and how often we shun personal responsibilities in the name of convention.

Another potential problem with casuistry is the tendency to cede moral authority to "ethical experts." Since good casuistry requires a fair bit of specific knowledge about traditions and paradigm cases, we may be tempted to defer to specially trained ethics consultants (Juengst, 1989). This would be a mistake and is unrealistic for several reasons. First, Jonsen and Toulmin (1988) have argued that "casuistry is unavoidable" in moral reasoning (p. 329). As we contemplate various difficult situations, our natural tendency is to think back to our previous experiences and our knowledge of similar cases. Not everyone has or needs training as a moral philosopher to reason casuistically, but it is important to recognize one's gaps in knowledge. Another problem with designating specific people "ethics experts" is the possibility of exacerbating casuistry's tendency to be an individualistic endeavor. Since Jonsen and Toulmin make a second claim for casuistry, "namely that moral knowledge is essentially particular," (p. 330) this indicates that all people can participate at some level of moral discourse. Consulting more experienced individuals to learn about paradigmatic cases can facilitate thoroughness but this does not suggest that one's own particular knowledge is any less valuable. In fact, the foundation of casuistry is shaken if we favor the technical knowledge about paradigm cases over specific knowledge about the case at hand. The challenge to all moral agents is the cultivation of the virtue *phronesis*, or moral wisdom, to guide moral reasoning. In the next chapter, we take up virtue ethics and explore its unique contributions to the moral life in relation to principlism and casuistry.

REFERENCES

Arras, J. D. (1991a). Getting down to cases: The revival of casuistry in bioethics. *The Journal of Medicine and Philosophy, 16*, 29-51.

Arras, J. D. (1994). Principles and particularity: The roles of cases in bioethics. *Indiana Law Journal, 69*, 983-1014.

Beauchamp, T. L., & Childress, J. F. (1994). *Principles of biomedical ethics* (4th ed.). NY: Oxford University Press.

Carson, R.A. (1986). Case method. *Journal of Medical Ethics, 12*, 36-38.

Childress, J. F. (1994). Principles-oriented bioethics: An analysis and assessment from within. In E. R. DuBose, R. Hamel, & L. J. O'Connell (Eds.), *A matter of principles: Ferment in U.S. bioethics* (pp. 72-98). Valley Forge, PA: Trinity Press International.

Frankena, W. (1973). *Thinking about morality*. Ann Arbor, MI: University of Michigan.

Gibbs, A. (1992). *Reconciling rights and responsibilities of colleges and students.* (ASHE-ERIC Higher Education Report No. 5). Washington, DC: Association for the Study of Higher Education.

Hugo, V. (1997). *Les Miserables*. (C. E. Wilbur, Trans.). NY: Knopf. (Original work published 1862).

Jonsen, A. R. (1986). Casuistry and clinical ethics. *Theoretical Medicine, 7*, 65-74.

Jonsen, A. R. (1991a). Of balloons and bicycles or the relationship between ethical theory and practical judgment. *The Hastings Center Report, 21*(5), 14-16.

Jonsen, A. R. (1991b). Casuistry as methodology in clinical ethics. *Theoretical Medicine, 12*, 295-307.

Jonsen, A. R. (1995). Casuistry. In Warren T. Reich (ed.), *Encyclopedia of bioethics* (revised ed., Vol. 1, pp. 344-350). NY: Macmillan.

Jonsen, A. R., & Toulmin, S. (1988). *The abuse of casuistry*. Berkeley: University of California Press.

Juengst, E. T. (1989). Casuistry and the locus of certainty in ethics. *Medical Humanities Review, 3*, 19-27.

Kaplin, W. A., & Lee, B. A. (1997). *A legal guide for student affairs professionals* (3rd ed.) San Francisco: Jossey-Bass.

Mill, J. S. (1962). Utilitarianism. In M. Warnock, (Ed.) *Utilitarianism, On Liberty, Essay on Bentham: Together with selected writings of Jeremy Bentham and John Austin* (pp. 251-321). Middlesex, England: Penguin.

Miller, R. B. (1994). Narrative and casuistry: A response to John Arras. *Indiana Law Journal, 69*, 1015-1019.

Miller v. State of New York, 487 N.Y.S.2d 115 (1985).

Mullins v. Pine Manor College, 389 Mass. Mass. 47, 449 N.E.2d 331 (1983).

Nash, R. J. (1997). Teaching ethics in the student affairs classroom. *NASPA Journal, 35*, 3-19.

Solomon, W. D. (1995). Ethics: Normative ethical theories. In Warren T. Reich (ed.), *Encyclopedia of bioethics* (Rev. ed., Vol. 2, pp. 736-748). NY: Macmillan.

Toulmin, S. (1981). The tyranny of principles. *The Hastings Center Report, 11*(6). 31-39.

Wicks, A. C., Spielman, B. J., & Fletcher, J. C. (1995). Survey of ethical orientations and theories. In J. C. Fletcher, C. A. Hite, P. A. Lombardo, & M. F. Marshall (Eds.), *Introduction to clinical ethics* (pp. 239-247). Frederick, MD: University Publishing Group.

Wildes, K.W. (1993). The priesthood of bioethics and the return of casuistry. *The Journal of Medicine and Philosophy, 18*, 33-49.

Williams, S. H. (1994). Bioethics and epistemology: A response to Professor Arras. *Indiana Law Journal, 69*, 1021-1026.

CHAPTER FIVE

Virtues-based Approaches to Ethics

with Leslie Rezac

For many people, *virtues* and *values* are the first words that come to mind when thinking about morality. The popularity of these concepts is reflected in the length of time that William Bennett's (1996) *The Book of Virtues* was on the best seller lists and the constant talk of family values in the media. Unlike discussions about general concepts, such as *moral principles* or *paradigm cases*, discussions about the virtues of honesty or loyalty seem familiar. Many parents try to teach their children to be good, long before the children understand the nature of moral laws and analogical reasoning. We often assess our friends and colleagues by their virtues or vices, such as loyalty, kindness, arrogance, dishonesty. Virtues manifest themselves in all of our lives, but some ethicists say that the cultivation of the virtues should be our primary moral concern. In Chapters Three and Four, we described two different ways to make moral judgments that drew on the principlist and case-based models. In this chapter, we will consider virtues-based approaches to ethics and inquire whether *character ethics* is an alternative to the more problem-oriented approaches like principlism and casuistry. *Should we think about morality in terms of rules versus virtues, or is it possible to separate these moral components? Can we really draw such tight distinctions among these three moral theories, or should we be more concerned with the passes connecting the mountains?*

OVERVIEW OF VIRTUES-BASED ETHICS

Even though principles- and case-based approaches to ethics have dominated the writings of moral philosophers in the last three hundred years, virtues captured the attention of Plato, Aristotle, and many other philosophers and theologians through the Middle Ages. The emphasis on the virtues lost its currency in the 18th century as philosophers like Kant sought a more objective grounding for morality. Jeremy Bentham, the father of utilitarianism, considered the virtues disorderly since they were not easily systematized. During post-Enlightenment attempts to find an objective, ahistorical, and rational justification for ethics, virtue ethics was relegated to a supplementary role in the determination of what is right or wrong. Conceptions of virtues shifted away from the Aristotelian ideal that held virtues as central to the goal of achieving our proper end of happiness. After the age of reason, rather than being the primary concern of morality, consideration of the virtues became secondary to the formulation of moral rules. This shift persisted well into the 20th century. A popular dictionary of philosophy published in the late 1970s did not even have entries for *virtue, virtues,* or *character* (Flew, 1979).

Despite this period of dormancy, virtue-based ethics awoke from its slumbers in the late 1950s, particularly with philosopher Elizabeth Anscombe's famous 1958 article that questioned the overemphasis on principlist and consequentialist approaches to ethics and called for their abandonment. Although she did not explicitly develop a virtues-based approach to ethics, Anscombe suggested that principlist and consequentialist methods be put aside in the interest of developing a more adequate moral psychology: "Eventually it might be possible to advance to considering the concept of virtue; with which, I suppose, we should be beginning some sort of a study of ethics" (Anscombe, 1958, p. 15). Her article triggered a renewed interest in virtue ethics that has continued, to this day, to provide novel perspectives for ethical discourse.

The recent revival of virtues-based ethics resulted from what some perceive as a void, an incompleteness, in our moral theories. Principles- and case-based ethics are seen as not doing justice to our moral sensibilities, often neglecting our deeply felt moral commitments, relationships, and habits. Reflecting on morality in terms of acts or circumstances accentuates the tendency to think about human actions in an atomistic manner. A principles-based approach may suggest a picture of life as a sequence of discrete actions that respond to conflicts and the need to resolve them. Even though principles-based ethics does not claim to represent the whole of moral life, this approach is geared toward the resolution of moral quandaries. Case-based methods in ethics also emphasize what we should do in particular contentious situations. Principlism and casuistry may offer two methods for helping us resolve conflicts, but now we must consider the rest of the moral life. In the introduction, we discussed the difference between everyday ethics and conflict-oriented ethics. Virtues-based ethics tries to combat the individualistic nature of problem-oriented ethics methods and to present a more unified approach to morality.

While principles- and case-based methods concentrate on specific decisions and rules, virtues-based approaches often look at an individual's moral development as a continuum and consider how particular communities come to value, develop, and establish their virtues. Virtues-based methods in ethics seek to present a vision for a more unified approach to ethics in our lives because "someone who possesses a virtue can be expected to manifest it in very different types of situations" (MacIntyre, 1984, p. 205).

This method also often considers how particular communities develop their virtues. In responding to students who are posting offensive materials, or to the students in "Do Your Part" who put up posters insulting an individual, Hauerwas (1995), a virtues-based ethicist, would begin evaluating the situation by asking questions that reflect relevant commitments: *What kind of individual performs such an act? What kind of a community allows its members to hurt each other in this way? What does it say about our community that we let this happen?* While a principle such as valuing autonomy may be a consideration for these communities, principles are not the first considerations in a virtues-based approach. Attention to rules or principles in individual cases tends to distort our moral vision, and we can lose sight of other trails and mountains, which reflect the questions asked above.

The most influential account of a virtues-based approach to ethics appears in Aristotle's *The Nichomachean Ethics* (1953), which was composed in the fourth century B.C.E. For Aristotle, the proper end of human life is called *eudaimonia*, a concept of happiness associated with the soul's realization of the species' essence; to live a virtuous life is to develop a character that is in accordance with that essence and that manifests itself in acts appropriate to it. Happiness is living a life according to the virtues by using our moral wisdom to perform acts that reflect a proper character. The moral virtues are products of habits, according to Aristotle, so we must practice certain kinds of actions in certain kinds of ways in order to develop and maintain virtues. In describing the relationship between the quality of the act and the character of the agent, Aristotle notes,

> *virtuous acts are not done in a just or temperate way merely because they have a certain quality, but only if the agent also acts in a certain state, viz. 1) if he knows what he is doing, 2) if he chooses it for its own sake, and 3) if he does it from a fixed and permanent disposition. (p. 97)*

This illustrates the tight link between action and agent and emphasizes the character of the agent as the primary concern of virtues-based ethics. In addition to his concern for the agent's character, Aristotle also established a central role for reason in his ethics by incorporating moral reflection and deliberation about actions. Reason, as expressed in the virtue prudence, functions as a *part* of this method rather than as its sole foundation, as in

Kantian philosophy. To have a virtue for Aristotle involves having the practical wisdom to determine what should be done in a concrete situation.

Following Aristotle's lead, contemporary virtue ethicists claim that *how* we perform certain acts is as important as *what* we do (Hauerwas, 1995, p. 2527). According to Aristotle (1953), "acts, to be sure, are called just and temperate when they are such as a just or temperate man would do; but what makes the agent just or temperate is not merely the fact that he does such things, but the fact that he does them in the way that just and temperate men do."(p. 98)

In "Do Your Part," the Resident Staff members were not only disturbed by the students' actions but by the students' attitudes, as manifested in the actions. When the students began to insult the Resident Staff members in person and on the posters, they were not acting kindly or with respect. Although the students were angry with the resident staff members, their actions did not have to manifest unkindness. Virtue ethics gives us a way of evaluating the motives and underlying character of agents. Perhaps the students did not intend to wound the Resident Staff members with their rhetoric but merely meant to rally other students around their cause. We cannot know the intentions of the students who used inflammatory language, but we can assess the kinds of character traits that lead to unkind actions.

This example shows us that when evaluating a situation, a virtues-based approach examines the character and motivation of the agents, not merely relevant principles or the potential consequences of their actions. Virtues-oriented moral imperatives like "Be loving" offer guidance about the way we ought to *be* rather than what we ought to *do* (Frankena, 1973, pp. 63ff). Principles- and case-based ethics can be categorized as *ethics of doing*, whereas a virtues-based approach is an *ethic of being*. This focus on the character of the agent is exemplified by the question *"What ought I be?"* More problem-based methods, on the other hand, ask, *"What ought I do?"* (Childress, 1994, p. 93). These two facets of morality are not mutually exclusive, for "being" involves "doing." The renowned philosopher William Frankena observes that "it must be remembered that 'being' involves at least trying to 'do.' Being without doing, like faith without works, is dead" (1973, p. 66). The students in Forman College felt the need to protest the implementation of the security policy, but the specific actions they took should have prompted questions like, *Is this the kind of person I want to be?*

Virtues-based ethics assesses the morality of a situation using characterizations such as *he was trustworthy* or *she was courageous*, rather than judging according to principles and rules. This represents a significant shift away from action- and consequences-oriented methods that seek to determine the *rightness* or *wrongness* of the acts.

> *Though any inherent features of actions or potential consequences certainly matter, what most concerns this tradition of ethics is how agents can cultivate and display their courage, temperance, charity, or other virtues through their relationships with others in a community.* (Wicks, Spielman, & Fletcher, 1995)

When we assess a situation from a virtues-based perspective, we are less concerned with the outward performance of an act than with the internal motives behind it. Rather than asking *Was this act right?* a virtue ethicist asks, *Is she a virtuous person?* Actions are expressions of an agent's character and are not deemed morally significant when divorced from considerations about the agent's character.

A virtues-oriented method of considering the situation described in "Do Your Part" would focus on the character of the individuals involved rather than on the nature of the acts themselves or the circumstances surrounding the case. Even though the Resident Staff members in Forman College violated the First Amendment rights of the students, someone functioning within a virtues-based approach would, perhaps, not judge the staff so harshly if their motives were good. Similarly, when the Resident Staff brought judicial charges against some of the students who had propped doors, a virtues-based assessment would examine the staff members' motives. It is not inherently moral or immoral to bring charges against a student for violating a policy, but the motives of the action shade our deliberations. We would feel differently if the staff members had acted out of revenge than if they had somewhat reluctantly enforced this university policy. In a virtues-based approach to ethics, there is no universal right or wrong response to a situation, because the character of the agent is the determining factor. Our judgment of moral acts depends on values such as those represented in the following syllogism: courage is a virtue; it is good to be virtuous; therefore it is good to be courageous.

How do virtue ethicists assess such intangible qualities as motive and character? A virtues-based approach to ethics involves three different components: a) developing a conception of the ideal person, b) developing a list of virtues needed to cultivate the ideal disposition, and c) defending a view about how to cultivate the virtues (Solomon, 1995, p. 739). The list of virtues is dependent on the development of *specific* ideal dispositions, which will vary according to the kind of person being considered: the ideal counselor may have different attributes from the ideal trial attorney. Robert Nash's (1997) list of virtues necessary for living as good democratic citizens, to be examined below, provides an example of such a list. We also explore questions about making moral judgments based on virtues-based ethics. *How do you know if someone is acting from the right motives? Is an agent's character really any of our concern as long as she does the right thing? How should we understand the relationship between being and doing?* Before we can tackle these more specific questions about virtues-based ethics, we must consider the definition of a virtue.

WHAT IS A VIRTUE?

The endurance of virtues-based ethics in a variety of forms of moral reflections, i.e., philosophical, religious, and literary, is in part attributable to the many definitions of *virtue*. Beauchamp and Childress note that several philosophers define a virtue as "a disposition to act or a habit of acting in accordance with moral principles, obligations, or ideals" (1994, p. 63). This definition is incomplete because it places virtues in a subordinate role to moral principles and neglects the importance of virtues in directing the agent's motives. "Properly motivated persons often do not merely follow rules; they also have a morally appropriate desire to act as they do" (Beauchamp & Childress, 1994, p. 64). Consider the following description of the motivational conception of virtues:

> *If we ask for guidance about what to do or not to do, then the answer is contained, at least primarily, in two deontic [duty-based] principles and their corollaries, namely the principles of beneficence and equal treatment [justice]. . . . We also know that we should cultivate two virtues, a disposition to be beneficial (i.e., benevolence) and a disposition to treat people equally (justice as a trait). But the point of acquiring these virtues is not further guidance or instruction; the function of the virtues in an ethics of duty is not to tell us what to do but to ensure that we will do it willingly in whatever situations we may face. In an ethics of virtue, on the other hand, the virtues play a dual role—they must not only move us to do what we do, they must also tell us what to do. (Frankena, 1973, pp. 66-67)*

What can virtues-based ethics tell us about the proper decision when faced with a moral conflict? From one perspective, virtues can determine the motives for certain actions but cannot themselves determine which actions are right (Childress, 1994, p. 94). Similarly, Frankena comments that principles alone are not sufficient for determining our actions:

> *Since morality cannot provide us with fixed principles of actual duty but only with principles of prima facie duty, it cannot be content with the letter of its law, but must foster in us the dispositions that*

will sustain us in the hour of decision when we are choosing between conflicting principles of prima facie duty or trying to revise our working rules of right and wrong. (Frankena, 1973, p. 66)

What relationship do you see between principles and virtues? Do you think that virtues provide the motivational component of actions, or can they help us determine what to do?

Frankena defines a virtue as a "disposition, habit, or trait of the person or soul, which an individual either has or seeks to have" (1973, p. 64). While this definition is quite elegant, it does not accurately reflect the historical differences in discussions about the nature of virtues. According to the philosopher Alasdair MacIntyre (1984), Homer understood a virtue as a quality that enables someone to perform what his well-defined social role required. Aristotle, on the other hand, thought that a virtue was a quality that led to the achievement of the human *telos* (or proper end), which was the good life. The New Testament also supports a teleological account of the virtues, despite different views about specific virtues. For Benjamin Franklin, even though the virtues were oriented to the end of happiness, utility was the criterion for meeting this end in particular cases (MacIntyre, 1984). These accounts of virtues differ according to the values of the community and of the individual providing the definition. Given this variety, if there is to be any coherent functioning of a virtues-based ethic, the conception of the virtuous person and the role of the community in developing the values embodied by such a person must be established. In the next section, we will examine the relationship between virtues and communities.

THE IDEAL MORAL PERSON AND THE IDEA OF COMMUNITY

In order to exemplify a virtuous moral character, we need some standard by which to measure ourselves. "For a virtue theory the question 'Which actions ought one to perform?' receives the response 'Those actions that would be performed by a perfectly virtuous agent." While a list of principles guides moral judgments in principles-based approaches, a picture of the ideal person and constitutive virtues guides virtues-based ethics (Solomon, 1995, p. 739). Creating a picture of the ideal person is part of our moral development because the ideals we accept help shape our character and motivate our actions.

> *Having a moral ideal involves wanting to be a person of a certain sort, wanting to have a certain trait of character rather than others, for example moral courage or perfect integrity. . . . Often such moral ideals of personality go beyond what can be demanded or regarded as obligatory, belonging among the things to be praised rather than required, except as one may require them of oneself. (Frankena, 1973, p. 67)*

Our pictures of those who embody moral ideals—such as Jesus, Martin Luther King, Jr., or Gandhi—not only provide a motivation to live a certain way but also present a guide for determining what such perfectly motivated actions may look like. Not all moral ideals entail supererogatory dispositions, such as those associated with saints and heroes; for some people, a grandmother or another wise person serves as a moral exemplar. These individuals demonstrate strength of character that compels admiration and emulation. Moral exemplars and the language of virtues-based ethics itself are ideal tools for self-revelation and formation (Nash, 1996, p. 65).

Given the proclivity of humans to model behavior on the virtuous or non-virtuous behavior of those viewed as authority figures, student affairs professionals should be aware of the potential effect and possible central role that their own manifested moral actions and character have on the students who may seek to imitate them. "Student affairs staff members probably can have a much greater impact on students' ethical development by modeling a concern for and adherence to a set of publicly owned standards than they ever could have when prescribing rigid rules for students" (Winston & McCaffrey, 1983, p. 185). Saints and heroes are not the only ones who embody moral ideals; each of us can display quality of character worthy of being said to represent an *ideal*. Students learn more about our values and character from the way we handle situations than from our words. Regardless of the approach to ethics we prefer, we all should cultivate an awareness of our potential roles as moral exemplars.

The concept of ideal persons was a part of the early development of colleges and universities. Moral character was a strong consideration in the selection of faculty members and presidents. President Hulbert of Middlebury College discussed the goal of education when he stated:

> *Men are in demand not homines, animals that wear pants, but vivi, plumed knights, with swords upon their thighs; scholars and specialists they may be, if back of scholarship and specialty there is manhood enough to bear up under them and put them to service. Men, I repeat, are in demand—men of independent and profound thought, of rational determined purposes, and of executive force. (Veysey, 1965, p. 29)*

This explicit reference to the importance of certain qualities of character reflects many of the societal values accepted in the early part of the twentieth century. This is not surprising, because conceptions of ideal persons are dependent on the societies that give them shape:

> *For Homer the paradigm of human excellence is the warrior; for Aristotle it is the Athenian gentleman. Indeed, according to Aristotle, certain virtues are only available to those of great riches and of high social status; there are virtues which are unavailable to the poor man, even if he is a free man. (MacIntyre, 1984, p. 182)*

MacIntyre notes that the New Testament praises virtues that Aristotle does not mention and sees riches as inimicable to virtue. Attempting to locate common ground among different accounts of virtues is futile given the wildly disparate traditions from which they emerge. This lack of a fixed catalog does not mean that we can discount consideration of the virtues. Instead, we should recognize the imbeddedness of virtues in their historical communities rather than try to find universal definitions. Building consensus about the nature of virtues occurs only within specific historical communities that hold shared values and understand how to express them. In "Do Your Part," we can see the impact of a community's values on the notion of virtue accepted by its members. Old State University had a strong tradition of respecting students' abilities to govern themselves; this tradition of self-governance required a degree of trustworthiness among the students. Another institution may have a culture that includes stronger remnants of *in loco parentis* and would not necessarily foster the same virtues as OSU.

MacIntyre (1984) observes that one of the major problems with contemporary society is that its diversity does not allow for a coherent overall scheme for morality. The diversity itself is not responsible for the lack of a common morality; rather, we are limited by our tendency to cling to remnants of morality from past cultures whose specific communities validated particular approaches to ethics. Essentially, we appropriate parts of morality from many eras, but our values do not necessarily reflect the underlying way of life of the community that first embraced these virtues. What we possess now are "the fragments of a conceptual scheme, parts which now lack those contexts from which their significance derived. We possess indeed simulacra of morality, we continue to use many of the key expressions" (MacIntyre, 1984, p. 2). Our society lacks the grounding of a common framework that would make it possible for philosophers, as well as others, to agree on an appropriate starting point. Finding some degree of agreement about the common good in a morally pluralistic society requires a renewed emphasis on community and on the political implications of ethics.

> *Such politics cannot be reduced to the struggle for power but, rather, is about the constitution of a community's habits for the production of a certain kind of people—that is, people who have the requisite virtues to sustain such a community (Hauerwas, 1995, p. 2527).*

Feminist scholar Marilyn Friedman (1989) highlights the political nature of communities and spells out their potential dangers. Communities of family, neighborhood, and nation play large roles in our moral development, but these communities have been oppressive to women over the years. Attention to the destructive and constructive elements of community is necessary to guard against these forms of oppression.

Unlike this emphasis on community in the development of moral virtues, Enlightenment theories of ethics assumed that an ahistorical approach to ethics was possible. Philosophers like Kant grounded their methods in ahistorical concepts, such as reason, and made the individual morally sovereign (Pence, 1984, p. 283). In the same way that virtues-based ethics discards an ahistorical approach to ethics, it also casts off the idea that morality involves faceless, nameless agents (Pincoffs, 1971). We are not dealing with universal situations or abstract people but with complex interactions between people and their environments:

> *We cannot describe the problem by describing an anonymous collision situation. Aristotle did not give open lectures; St. Paul did not write open letters. When they used the word 'we,' they spoke from within a community of expectations and ideals: a community within which character was cultivated (Pincoffs, 1971, p. 570).*

The word *community* carries many different connotations, but we favor the definition proposed by Robert Brown (1985): "a community is a gathering of people with similar concerns and common goals who share a mutual interest in assisting or supporting one another" (p. 70). Each college or university may be considered a community with its own set of moral ideals, each institution founded on different principles with different goals for its community.

> *Of course the busiest agents of all this college founding were the religious denominations—some more than others, some later than others, but few were not involved. They worked in an environment of national ambition, democratic aspiration, geographic isolation, and romantic imagination, and state by state they turned their own rivalries into sets of competing colleges. (Rudolph, 1962, p.54)*

Public institutions have a strong commitment to public service whereas colleges or universities founded through religious orders have a different set of goals.

> *A college develops a sense of unity where, in a society created from many of the nations of Europe, there might otherwise be aimlessness and uncontrolled diversity. A college advances learning; it combats ignorance and barbarism. A college is useful: it helps men to learn the things they must know in order to manage the temporal affairs of the world; it trains a legion of teachers (Rudolph, 1962, p. 13).*

Even within each college or university community, smaller communities exist. An example of this in "Do Your Part" is Forman College and the Resident Staff Program. These two smaller communities existed within the larger community of OSU, yet each had different ideals that held them together. As long as the values of these two communities did not conflict, they could coexist peacefully within the larger OSU community; however, when the mores of one community came into conflict with the other, the integrity of each was tested. In "Do Your Part," the students considered Forman College a community where the virtues of independence, autonomy, and loyalty were critical to its communal culture. The individuals who lived there may have considered it necessary to sue the administration in order to maintain the virtues which were central to the community's identity.

What are the characteristics of the community where you live? Do you share its values, or do you think they are somewhat distorted? What values do the communities within your institution reflect? Who are the moral exemplars and what are their virtues?

WHAT MAY A LIST OF VIRTUES INCLUDE?

Just as there are many ways to describe virtues, there also are many ways to judge what dispositions are virtuous. If we are pure egoists, then any traits that enhance our own welfare are good. If an individual has a more utilitarian orientation, then any virtue that promotes the general good is valued. Another view holds that certain virtues are inherently good, regardless of their contribution to an individual's well-being or to the welfare of others. From this perspective, virtue is its own reward rather than the means to an end. The community's list of virtues will reflects its values and determine its approach to the virtuous citizen or member. Therefore, "the fundamental ethical question . . . remains a question about the correct set of virtues for human beings" (Solomon, 1995, p. 739).

Holism, humanism, and individualism have been identified as cornerstone values of the student affairs profession (Winston & McCaffrey, 1983, pp. 175-177). Values such as these are reflected in lists of virtues that mirror the values of specific communities. *Do you think these values still influence the field of student affairs administration? If so, what virtues would best express these values?* A list of some virtues valued by many communities includes wisdom, temperance, courage, loyalty, generosity, charity, justice, and tolerance. Virtues such as these combine to characterize moral ideals. Moral agents acquire a mix of these virtues and many others based on their communities. Such lists of virtues, based on the moral exemplars held by a particular community, help us to assess a virtuous disposition.

Robert Nash addresses some of the problems in developing a rich conception of the virtues in a pluralistic, morally ambiguous culture. Renewed interest in character education has sparked a cottage industry of manuals concerned with moral development of "good character." Nash notes that these texts lack practical and pedagogical substance (Nash, 1997). His antidote to some of the dangers accompanying moral pluralism is to promote a general virtue curriculum for school and universities that commit themselves to the cultivation of a "democratic character." Given the diversity of opinions and beliefs in our society, Nash (1997) stresses that people need certain skills to deliberate collectively and reach compromises about complicated issues.

> *Educators should commit themselves to the cultivation of a "democratic character" among citizens, one that effectively predisposes people to engage in collective decision making; respect liberty, autonomy, and political equality; and reach consent through careful deliberation.*
>
> *Beyond mere rote knowledge of laws, constitutions, and political institutions, certain virtues are necessary for democratic citizens to become truly self-governing. What citizens require is a certain liberality of character, marked by the virtues of self-discipline, obligation, civility, tolerance, fairness, and generosity. (p. 11)*

Nash's list grows out of his values for a democratic community and the virtues needed to develop a responsible citizenry, but it offers us only one example of how communal values shape the virtues of its members. With this specific list in mind, we must try to understand how particular members of a community acquire the virtues on this list. *How does the community set about developing and instilling the virtues on such a list?*

TEACHING MORAL VIRTUES

How do you go about trying to persuade another person to be a certain way?
> *The challenge then is to move students and the campus community not back to the superimposed responsibility and dedication. How can we raise student awareness of social and ethical issues to new levels? How can we foster commitment to fundamental values so that our vast knowledge will be used in a more just, decent, humane, and civilized way? (McBee, 1994, p. 571)*

This challenge is faced by any community that holds its members to a particular set of standards. Laws can function to sanction specific behaviors, such as murder, trespassing, and theft, but *how can a community have or enforce a law requiring citizens to be courageous?* Critics of virtues-based ethics argue that one cannot teach virtue. *How do you feel about such a criticism? What constitutes moral education? How can a community facilitate its members' acquisition of the list of virtues it values?* Plato and Aristotle were both concerned with the question, "Who can tell whether virtue is acquired by teaching or practice, or if neither teaching nor practice, does it come about by some other way?" (Nash, 1997, p. 36).

Proponents of the neo-classical education model seek to reinvigorate moral education with attention to Aristotelian and Platonic notions of the virtues. Yet, some scholars question whether we really are in such a state of moral decline and whether virtue educators are any better equipped to teach character development than others. Vesting this authority in the schools and their virtue educators runs the "risk of establishing a moral character elite whereby only a privileged group possesses virtue and is alone qualified to foster it" (Nash, 1997, p. 37). It is naïve to think that schools can reverse the long-term effects of family and community on a student's character. The ubiquitous cultural messages sent by television, movies, and printed media insure that is nearly impossible to reshape character through formal education.

We are assuming in this discussion of virtue-education that learning to be virtuous just involves acquiring specific virtues; these traits are not hardwired into us or transmitted to us by a divinity. Unlike rules and paradigm cases, we cannot just consult a canon of virtues, memorize them, and start acting virtuously. Instead,

> *Important sources for virtue ethicists rather than taking the form of rules or codes are narratives, stories, and biographies which illustrate and embody a virtuous way of life so that people can imitate their example, just as a young apprentice learns a craft from studying under a skilled carpenter. What makes one a true artisan has far more to do with imitation and a gradual development of good judgments, habits, and practices which are shaped over time than it does with learning a series of rules or following a set of directions.* (Wicks, Spielman & Fletcher, 1995, p. 241)

For Aristotle, a lifelong process of cultivating proper habits was the key to developing virtues. Everytime we make a decision between telling the truth or telling a white lie, we develop habits about truth-telling that shape our virtues. If we are in the habit of telling white lies for convenience or to "spare someone's feelings," we must ask whether we really are trying to protect the other person or whether lying represents cowardice or an unwillingness to face conflict. These sorts of questions and this kind of vigilance can help us examine the habits expressed by our actions, allowing the opportunity to develop our character.

This emphasis on the gradual development of virtues and their reshaping over time also reminds us that "an aim of moral education, likely to be overlooked by quandrists, is the development of the sense of the moral self as the product of continuous cultivation" (Pincoffs, 1971, p. 567). Just as we can acquire the virtue of honesty, we can also lose it by lying or cheating on a regular basis. Like other skills, virtues can become rusty: "If the moral virtues are acquired habits rather than innate gifts, it is always possible that one can lose relative proficiency in these habits" (Louden, 1984, p. 231). We cannot just assume that a good person always will do the right thing, because even the most virtuous person can act "out of character" (Louden, 1984, p. 229).

Aristotle makes the point that anyone can make the kind of mistake from which tragedies result, regardless of their character, and virtue ethics lacks any way to evaluate these tragic outcomes. For example, Oedipus unknowingly killed his father and had sexual relations with his mother; when he discovered the true nature of his acts, he suffered tremendously, despite his good motives and character. Louden offers the following comments on the relationship between virtues and actions in tragic situations:

> *My point is that virtue ethics is in danger of blinding itself to the wrongful conduct in Oedipal acts, simply because it views the Oedipuses of the world as honorable persons and because its focus is on long term character manifestations rather than on discrete acts... This is not to say that virtue ethics does not ever address the issue of right and wrong action, but rather that it can only do so in a derivative manner. Sometimes, however, it is clearly acts rather than agents that ought to be the primary focus of moral evaluation.* (Louden, 1984, pp. 230, 232)

Someone evaluating Oedipus from within a virtues-based framework would think that his ignorance at the time of the actions would allow us to label his actions *tragic*. By contrast, someone operating from a strictly rules-based approach may see these as evil acts in spite of the mitigating circumstances. Tragedy is on the fringe of the moral life, so we will not dwell on whether tragic acts can be morally excused. Our intent in drawing on Louden's discussion is to illustrate the tension between virtue and the need to assess the morality of discrete acts.

While the difficulty of assessing discrete acts poses some problems for virtues-based ethics, it also highlights one of the major strengths of this method. Attention to our character over time helps preserve virtues when we perform acts with proper motives, and it also gives us a sense of the continuity of our moral lives. Virtues-based ethics helps to reduce the frequency of atomistic thinking in our lives. We often see ourselves in different roles (father, dean, coach, etc.) and may feel disjointed as we try to fulfill all of our responsibilities. Roles often come with expectations about how those occupying them ought to act in particular situations (Nash, 1996). This normative component of roles tells us what we ought to do and may require different virtues in order to fulfill all of our responsibilities (for example, a virtue of a coach may be competitiveness, but this would not be as highly valued in a dean). In addition to these role-specific virtues, virtues-based ethics also allows us to examine the different shapes that a virtue like compassion takes in our lives. Compassion, honesty, and many other virtues are desirable in all people, regardless of their different roles, but these virtues may be expressed in any number of ways. The virtue of caring allows a mother to draw her child into her lap and comfort him when he is hurt, but expressing caring in this way with a student would be unacceptable. Virtues-based ethics allows deep and dynamic understandings of the moral virtues, but it can also lead to confusion and inappropriate actions when the agents do not possess the moral wisdom to alter their expression of the virtues for different situations. *Do you think that different roles require different virtues? How would you characterize these differences? What virtues do you think cross professional and personal lines? Do you feel these distinctions in your life?*

PRACTICAL CONSIDERATIONS AND CRITICISMS

The skills and knowledge base needed to prepare for the profession of student affairs have received ample attention in the literature; however, it is worth considering whether there are certain virtues that might make student affairs professionals more successful. For example, *The Student Learning Imperative* recommends that "Student affairs professionals collaborate with other institutional agents and agencies to promote student learning and personal development" (ACPA, 1994, p. 120). This suggests that student affairs professionals who possess virtues that foster collaboration may be better able to achieve appropriate goals. If an individual is known to be cooperative and open-minded, *do you think she would be more likely to succeed as a student affairs professional than someone who did not possess these traits?*

Incorporating a virtues-based approach to ethics into their professional lives presents unique challenges to those in students affairs. The challenging task of understanding and developing moral character can mitigate the sense of leading a segmented life and may remind us that we can never turn off our character. Whether we like it or not, when we perform specific actions, we send a message about our moral character. Virtues-based ethics suggests reflection upon our acquired virtues and the ways they motivate our actions so that the message we send really reflects our character. As intentional or unintentional mentors to students and colleagues, we have the responsibility to develop an awareness of the virtues we value and of the ways they are expressed (or not) in our own lives.

Mentoring and the development of habits are two main processes for developing moral character, yet effecting change through each requires a significant investment of time and skill (Batchelor, 1995). We must ask ourselves whether college-aged students are capable of character changes that are mediated by another person. Nash cites several studies that indicate that a healthy skepticism about teaching moral character is warranted, given the complex factors influencing character development. An awareness of the difficulties of shaping moral character and of the profundity of this task suggests that we proceed with "caution and humility whenever we attempt to teach the virtues" (Nash, 1997, p. 51).

In addition to the difficulties inherent in trying to teach someone to be virtuous, we also encounter difficulties assessing the character of moral agents. For example, *doing the right thing for the wrong reason would be blameworthy for a virtue ethicist, but how do we know that a person has acted with wrong reasons?* Conversely, doing the wrong thing for the right reasons (for example, killing someone in the name of justice) presents its own problems. Virtue ethics seems to lack any external ways to evaluate moral acts because the focus is shifted away from the nature of acts themselves or their consequences (Louden, 1984). *Is it reasonable to expect other people to know our motives and judge us accordingly?* If this is the only method for assessing praise and blame in a situation, we are faced with a very difficult task as student affairs professionals. Either we must rely on an individual's reports about her motives, or we need a long-term perspective on the agent's actions. The long-term perspective may reveal patterns of moral conduct that can help us assess the agent's motives. Given the relatively quick turnover of students, however, this option is particularly unlikely for student affairs professionals.

Critics often charge that virtues-based ethics is too rooted in historical communities and therefore it lacks a "reliable yardstick." Robert Louden notes that for the Greeks, pride, in moderation, was considered a virtue, whereas the New Testament values humility. What is considered a virtue or vice is tradition-dependent. Some critics who accept this strong dependence on tradition note that modern cultures are so pluralistic that it would be nearly impossible to identify a common set of values that are able to inform our public ideas about the virtues and vices. Unlike Aristotle's Athens, which was small and had a homogeneous population, many contemporary communities incorporate varied cultural traditions that may value different virtues.

Some feminists argue that even virtues-based ethics is still too individualistic. Although this approach includes explicit reference to the communal webs of human social life, it still focuses exclusively on the moral development of the individual.

> *[Virtue theory] requires, then, merely that an agent develop justice. There is nothing in [virtue theory] itself that requires an agent to bring about justness in others.*
>
> *A virtue theory gives agents reasons to act because it is supposed that each person wants to be a flourishing and fulfilled human being. An agent's own life and character then will have a certain primacy according to a virtue theory. (Solomon, 1995, pp. 741-742)*

In the conclusion, we will explore Margaret Urban Walker's (1988) feminist approach to ethics, one that emphasizes our responsibilities to others. Clearly, an ethic of responsibility may encourage the development of virtues that nurture a sense of connection to others; many supporters of a virtues-based ethics have placed an emphasis on building the agent's moral character, with social and personal responsibilities treated as matters of secondary importance.

Can virtues-based ethics or the other ethical approaches we have discussed escape these criticisms about their function? Perhaps the key is not to focus on one theory, because each seems to be incomplete or problematic. To properly traverse the moral landscape one must, perhaps, find a pass that connects the various theories rather than one that leads straight up one of the particular peaks.

THE PASSES . . .

William Frankena proposes "that we regard the morality of duty and principles and the morality of virtues or traits of character not as rival kinds of morality between which we must choose, but as two complementary aspects of the same morality" (Frankena, 1973, p. 65). For every principle that prescribes right action, there will be a morally good trait that leads to a disposition to act according to the principle (Frankena, 1973). Granted, Frankena makes other comments in his book that make virtues derivative of principles; however, we agree with his statement that it is unnecessary to view virtues-based ethics and quandary ethics as wholly distinct. Perhaps we can understand their interaction as dialectical: as we further refine our understanding of our moral principles, our character is enhanced, and this enhancement allows us to understand more deeply the obligations presented by principles. When working with a virtues-based approach, we learn that when we make moral decisions we do not simply *do* something. We can also affirm (or negate) our long-term values and can shape our moral character in new ways (Nash, 1996).

> *While I do think that contemporary virtue ethicists are correct in asserting that any adequate moral theory must account for the fact of character, and that no ethics of rules, pure and unsupplemented, is up to this job . . .[my] analysis also suggests that no ethics of virtue, pure and unsupplemented, can be satisfactory.* (Louden, 1984, p. 235)

Perhaps we can hold virtues as ideals for which we should strive and principles as side constraints on our actions. In a recent article, Jane Fried (1997) reaffirms Hughes' (1992) contention that principles and virtues interact in the context of complex communities to inform our moral decision making. As a profession, we must challenge our own complacency about the ethical principles that have served us in dealing with a more homogenous student community and begin to examine the multiple values and belief systems on which our current students are basing their lives. In the conclusion, we will offer a method that attempts to synthesize the demands of these components within the narratives of our personal and communal lives.

REFERENCES

American College Personnel Association. (1994). *The student learning imperative: Implications for student affairs*. Washington, DC: Author.

Anscombe, G. E. M. (1958). Modern moral philosophy. *Philosophy 33*(no. 124), 1-19.

Aristotle. (1953). *The ethics of Aristotle: The Nichomachean ethics* (J. A. K. Thompson, Trans.). Middlesex, England: Penguin Books.

Batchelor, S. W. (1993). Mentoring and self-directed learning. In M. J. Barr & Associates (Eds.). *Handbook of student affairs administration* (pp. 378-389). San Francisco, CA: Jossey-Bass.

Beauchamp, T. L., & Childress, J. F. (1994). *Principles of biomedical ethics* (4th ed.). NY: Oxford.

Bennett, W. J. (1996). *The book of virtues: A treasury of great moral stories*. NY: Simon & Schuster.

Brown, R. D. (1985). Creating an ethical community. In H. J. Canon & R. D. Brown (Eds.), *Applied ethics in student services* (pp. 67-79). San Francisco: Jossey-Bass.

Childress, J. F. (1994). Principles-oriented bioethics: An analysis and assessment from within. In E. R. DuBose, R. Hamel, & L. J. O'Connell (Eds.), *A matter of principles: Ferment in U.S. bioethics* (pp. 72-98). Valley Forge, PA: Trinity Press International.

Frankena, W. (1973). *Thinking about morality*. Ann Arbor, MI: University of Michigan.

Flew, A. (1979). *A dictionary of philosophy*. (2nd ed.). NY: St. Martin's Press.

Fried, J. (1997). Changing Ethical Frameworks for a Multicultural World. In J. Fried (Ed.) *Ethics for today's campus: New perspective on education, student development, and institutional management*. (New Directions for Student Services, no. 77). San Francisco: Jossey-Bass.

Friedman, M. (1989). Feminism and modern friendship: Dislocating the community. *Ethics, 99*, 275-290.

Hauerwas, S. (1995). Virtue and character. In W. T. Reich (ed.), *Encyclopedia of bioethics* (Rev. ed., pp. 2525-2532). NY: Macmillan.

Louden, R. B. (1984) On some vices of virtue ethics. *American Philosophical Quarterly 21*, 227-236.

MacIntyre, A. (1984). *After virtue: A study in moral theory.* Notre Dame, IN: University of Notre Dame Press.

McBee, M. L. (1994). Moral development: From direction to dialogue. In Rentz, A. L. (Ed.), *Student affairs: A profession's heritage* (pp, 567-574). Lanham, Maryland: University Press of America.

Nash, R. J. (1996). *"Real world" ethics: Frameworks for educators and human service professionals.* NY: Teacher's College Press.

Nash, R. J. (1997). *Answering the "virtuecrats": A moral conversation on character education.* NY: Teacher's College Press.

Pence, G. E. (1984). Recent work on virtues. *American Philosophical Quarterly 21,* 281-297.

Pincoffs, E. L (1971). Quandary ethics. *Mind 80,* 552-571.

Rudolph, F. (1962). *The American college and university.* NY: Vintage.

Solomon, W. D. (1995). Ethics: normative ethical theories. In Warren T. Reich (ed.), *Encyclopedia of bioethics* (revised ed., Vol. 2, pp. 736-748). NY: Macmillan.

Veysey, L. R. (1965). *The emergence of the American university.* Chicago: The University of Chicago Press.

Walker, M.U. (1998). *Moral understandings: A feminist study in ethics.* NY: Routledge.

Wicks, A. C., Spielman, B. J., & Fletcher, J. C. (1995). Survey of ethical orientations and theories. In J. C. Fletcher, C. A. Hite, P. A. Lombardo, & M. F. Marshall (Eds.), *Introduction to clinical ethics* (pp. 239-247). Frederick, MD: University Publishing Group.

Winston, R. B., & McCaffrey, S. S. (1983). Ethical practice in student affairs administration. In T. K. Miller, R. B. Winston, Jr. & W. R. Mendenhall (Eds.), *Administration and leadership in student affairs: Actualizing student development in higher education* (pp. 167-191). Muncie, Indiana: Accelerated Development.

CHAPTER SIX

Conclusion: An Ethic of Responsibility

Now that we have become acquainted with the terrain of three mountains on the moral landscape, we realize that some readers may be thinking, "I don't like hiking in this mountain range; I prefer a different kind of mountain." The three approaches to ethics we present are meant to serve as guides for further reflection on the role of ethics in our personal and professional lives. When we learn morality, Margaret Urban Walker observes, "we learn who we are, to whom we are connected, and what matters enough to care about and care for" (1998, p. 201). Regardless of how we may describe our primary moral method, all of us encounter rules, cases, and virtues in our daily lives. Even if we do not use principlist, casuist, or virtue ethics methods, our colleagues or loved ones may use them.

Reflection on our moral lives may involve a process of trial and error before we find the best language to describe our moral methods. Discovering the moral language that best suits us is important because "mutual moral accounting must use shared terms that allow us to make sense of ourselves to each other" (Walker, 1998, p. 202). In the field of student affairs administration, Kuh (1996) notes:

> A common language must be developed to create and communicate what is to be accomplished (i.e., the shared vision), to discuss what factors contribute to student learning, to examine mental models

> *productively, and to view all this from the 'big picture,' or systemic frame of reference. (p. 139)*

As we work to discover this moral language, the following questions may serve as helpful catalysts: *Which of the ethical theories appeals to you the most? Do you have a preference among the theories, or does each seem to be applicable in particular situations? How would you rank the role that these theories play in your life? Can you describe the kinds of conflicts that may arise between someone who focuses on rules and someone who is more interested in virtues? How may these approaches function in everyday situations? Are some better suited to routine circumstances than others?*

In many ways, developing a framework for regular moral reflection is like developing a budget. Just as ethical concerns permeate all of our encounters with other people, concern with finances pervades our personal or professional lives. Spending money can be a carefully controlled and monitored activity or a haphazard endeavor (or a little bit of both). Sometimes we are prompted to design a budget because we face the crisis of a monetary shortfall. Other times, we spontaneously reflect on our use of money and realize that we would benefit from developing a budget. So, we sit down and examine our spending and earning patterns and work out a plan for the future. This involves setting priorities for the various components of our lives, i.e., groceries versus car payments versus vacations, and ordering them to reflect our goals. Preventive ethics is like developing a moral budget. We have to ask, *What is important to me and how do I try to enact these values in my life? What are my patterns in working with other people? Do I have a haphazard approach or a well-considered sense of the kind of professional I want to be?*

A moral budget also requires regular monitoring in order to make sure that we remain within its limits. Devising a budget is useless if we never look at it again and do not try to compensate when we exceed its limits. After three months, you may look back at your household budget and realize that you underestimated the amount of money you spend on groceries. The best solution in this case may be to increase the allotment of money for groceries and perhaps decrease that spent on fast food. With a moral budget, if you think that you favor virtues-based ethics, look at the last interactions you have had in your office and try to analyze their components. Do any of them involve attempts to be fair, honest, loyal, or whatever virtues resonate with you? If not, you have two options: try to change your behavior in the future to reflect your stated moral values, or re-evaluate your moral budget. Perhaps you do not really function in terms of virtues-based ethics but as a casuist. Neither approach is necessarily better than the other; each merely reflects different moral values. Once you have a sense of the ethics approach that best suits you, it is important to review it regularly to see if it still reflects your moral values. A moral budget is not an inflexible tool but a living and changing guide to provide accountability to ourselves and others. Both budgetary processes require constant examination, and possibly revision, in order to effectively serve as guides in our lives.

This analogy does not hold at every level because morality is not a limited resource like money (even though some virtues like *caring* do require careful allocation so we do not get burned out). We use this analogy to demonstrate some of the formal elements of working with ethical methods in our daily lives. Every dollar we spend is part of a budget (even if we categorize it as *miscellaneous funds*) and every interaction we have with others has ethical components. Ethics can use its many tools to offer a language for self-reflection, show potential areas of discontinuity, and help us understand conflicts, but it is more than a tool to resolve conflicts. It permeates all aspects of the field of student affairs and thus concerns the everyday issues that student affairs administrators encounter when dealing with each other and with students.

As indicated throughout this text, we do not believe that it is possible or desirable to maintain a strict separation among the three ethical methods we discussed. When navigating these moral mountains, we spend much time in the passes that connect the individual mountains. In Chapter Three, we noted that a principles-based ethics needs virtue ethics, and, in Chapter Four, we explored the role for principles in casuistry. In this last chapter, we bring the concerns of these three moral mountains together in a responsibility-based ethics. An ethics of responsibility has many different philosophical sources, including the work of H. Richard Niebuhr (1963), but it has been revived and redirected by a number of feminist thinkers, many of whom draw on and further develop, though not uncritically, Carol Gilligan's ground-breaking *In A Different Voice*, which was first published in 1982.

In most principles- and case-based moral methods (sometimes lumped together as justice perspectives), moral agents are seen first as individuals; their relations to each other are a secondary concern. In contrast, feminist ethics describes different kinds of moral experiences and intuitions that more accurately reflect the concerns of women but that have often been neglected in major approaches to ethics. Recognizing deficiencies in Lawrence Kohlberg's stages of moral development, Carol Gilligan heard a different moral "voice" in the young women she interviewed: they understood moral agents as essentially relational rather than as discrete individuals. Based on this work, many feminists have developed accounts of care as central to their moral models (Baier, 1987; Held, 1987, 1993; Manning, 1992; Noddings, 1984; Ruddick, 1989; Tronto, 1993). These varieties of the ethics of care attend to the concerns and responsibilities of women in their relationships with others and communities. Many sharply contrast the ethics of care with justice orientations to ethics that seem overly rationalistic as well as overly individualistic—an ethics of care emphasizes the affections and emotions that are often downplayed by other approaches (though care could be considered a virtue). Yet, Gilligan holds that justice and care orientations do not correlate strictly with gender—both women and men may hold either orientation—and that these two orientations are not mutually exclusive. Instead, Gilligan views these two orientations as "different ways of organizing the basic elements of moral judgment: self, others, and the relationship between them" (Gilligan, 1987, pp. 22-23; see also Carse, 1991, p. 6).

Although significant differences exist among various accounts of feminist ethics, some basic tenets are widely shared: a) criticisms of abstract theories and claims for objectivity; b) recognition of the role for concrete, contextual sources of knowledge rooted in socially situated subjects; c) concepts of reason that include feelings and emotions; d) recognition of the demands of relationships; e) openness to new forms of moral discourse; and f) the goal of the genuine liberation of women (Lebacqz, 1995, p. 812). With the ethics of responsibility, we present an approach to ethics that reflects many of these concerns of feminist ethics. It also best expresses and illuminates our day-to-day encounters with other people.

Along the way we noted the overly individualistic tendencies of each ethics approach explicated in this text, particularly in light of feminist critiques. Although principles-, case-, and virtues-based ethics (to varying degrees) account for the individual in his or her communities, the ethics of responsibility reflects a stronger sense of relationship than the other three theories. This approach begins with the view that all beings are interconnected and that these connections bring certain responsibilities. Instead of asking, first of all, to which principles and rules we should adhere, or which precedent cases we should follow, or which consequences we should produce, or which virtues we should develop, the ethics of responsibility asks, *what are my responsibilities in light of my relationships to others?* It is concerned with *to whom* and *for what* we are responsible.

Margaret Urban Walker (1998) develops an "expressive-collaborative" approach to an ethics of responsibility. She characterizes moral theories like principles- and case-based ethics as "theoretical-juridical" models that represent morality as a compact, action-guiding code. Finding the individualistic and impersonal tendencies of these models unsatisfactory, Walker presents an alternative model: morality is "a socially embodied medium of mutual understanding and negotiation between people over their responsibility for things open to human care and response" (1998, p. 9). This "expressive-collaborative" model pursues an equilibrium that can be characterized as a process of continuing negotiation among people regarding their responsibilities. Stated simply, the content of this model is to track responsibilities.

Essentially, then, morality is a matter of responsibility and accountability to particular people in particular situations given the intricate relationships among them. We learn about our responsibilities from our interactions with other people and sustain them through a constant process of evaluation. This continual feedback includes subtle, disapproving glances from a friend when we shirk responsibilities or even more direct attempts to make us accountable for our commitments. Critical reflection facilitates this process by helping us explore "who gets to do what to whom and who must do what for whom, as well as who has standing to give or to demand account" (Walker, 1998, p. 11).

By locating morality in practices of responsibility, Walker shifts its locus from actions and circumstances to the complex fabric of interactions among humans we encounter every day. Virtues-based ethics also moves from actions to the agent but still remains somewhat individualistic, despite its attention to community. Walker's method involves a constructive process of assigning responsibilities within communities, but it does not necessarily tell us how to fulfill these responsibilities.

> *The basic claim about the structure of responsibility is this: Specific moral claims on us arise from our contact with others whose interests are vulnerable to our actions and choices. We are obligated to respond to particular others when circumstances or ongoing relationships render them especially, conspicuously, or peculiarly dependent on us. This kind of ethics requires a view of moral judgment with significant expressive, interpretive, and (where possible) collaborative features. (Walker, 1998, p. 107)*

Not only do we have responsibilities to our families, co-workers, students, and friends, but we may also have responsibilities to strangers if our actions affect them. We thus have "moving horizons of commitments" which require our ethic of responsibility to balance flexibility with reasonable reliability (Walker, 1997, p. 66).

In "Do Your Part," the student affairs administrators had certain responsibilities to the staff members and to the students in Forman College. Protecting the safety of the students was certainly one responsibility, *but did the administrators also have a responsibility to address the students' concerns about the policy implementation in a more collaborative manner? Do you think professional and personal responsibilities differ in nature? If so, how would you describe this difference?*

Walker's expressive-collaborative method also focuses on the responsibilities of individuals within larger communities that have often displayed various prejudices and embodied patterns of discrimination, particularly against women and other marginalized groups. According to Walker, morality has social and political features. Indeed, "morality is a dimension of actual social lives that inheres in a society's ways of reproducing its members' senses of responsibility" (Walker, 1998, p. 203). The deep intertwining of our moral and social worlds has profound implications for the ways we understand our responsibilities to ourselves and to others. It is evident daily at the level of our communities. While these communities connect us to each other and shape our moral development, they also "harbor social roles and structures which have been highly oppressive for women" and other marginalized groups (Friedman, 1989, p. 103). Where there is a disparity of power, for instance, between men and women, it is necessary to examine morality in political terms if we hope to reshape our communal discourse (Tronto, 1993, p. 3).

The ethics of responsibility implicitly draws on the three ethical approaches presented in this text. In effect, it incorporates their major themes into a more comprehensive framework. Principles-based approaches offer some guidelines for how we can fulfill our responsibilities, particularly to relative strangers, and these principles provide a way to articulate the terms of our accountability. Consider, for example, the relationship between Helen (the head resident) and the residents of Forman College. Her responsibilities to them grew out of her role as head resident in the area and as their peer. In negotiating their relationship, including their commitments to each other, they had different perceptions of Helen's responsibility to the students. From the students' perspectives, the principle of personal autonomy suggested by Beauchamp and Childress (1994) offers one way to describe the breach of her responsibility to them. From Helen's perspective, however, the principle of non-maleficence describes the responsibilities the students had to each other but failed to actualize when they disregarded the security policy.

While such principles may help us understand the responsibilities within the relationship between Helen and the students, virtue ethics also contributes to the ethics of responsibility. In the community of Forman College, students understood, in general, that the privilege of self-governance brought certain responsibilities. Some virtues valued in their community were trustworthiness, and reliability since a great deal of responsibility for their living area was placed with the students. These character traits and many others are essential for a community to function and for its members to fulfill their responsibilities to each other. When the security policy was enacted in the College, the resident staff members relied on the trustworthiness of the students and hoped they would voluntarily follow the policy; however, the students violated this trust and the new policy by regularly disregarding it and propping the doors open. Conversely, the students could argue that resident staff administrators violated their trust by developing a policy with little input by Forman College's student government. Virtue ethics thus helps illuminate aspects of an ethics of responsibility that depends on the character of the agents and its impact on their ability to meet their commitments.

If people are lazy, mean, and selfish, they may have difficulty responding to the needs of those around them. For example, some students in Forman College may have propped the doors because they were lazy, not because they wanted to affirm the importance of student self-governance. Such disregard for the safety of other students is not acceptable, and the ethics of responsibility may need to draw on precedent cases in order to sanction the individuals. Case-based ethics, specifically casuistry, draws on past experiences within the community to help us reflect on this case. Perhaps we would look to previous cases of negligence to decide how to respond to members of the community who fail to meet their responsibilities.

In addition to this retrospective approach, we could also employ the future-oriented perspective of consequentialism. Within the ethics of responsibility, agents accept the responsibility for the intended and unintended consequences of their actions. The student who lazily props the door does not intend to allow a rapist to enter the residence hall, but, nonetheless, she is responsible if such a consequence occurs. While we may not be able to predict all of the consequences of our actions, it is helpful to focus on the ones that appear possible and probable as we attempt to fulfill our responsibilities.

The ethics of responsibility is rooted in relationships, but, as feminists and others remind us, some relationships are themselves unethical. Some are oppressive and have a negative impact on different groups as well as on particular individuals. It is important not to ignore oppressive patterns in university and college cultures. *What impact do our approaches to morality have on the position of traditionally marginalized groups, such as women and African Americans?* Attending to such questions can make the ethics of responsibility more aware of power differentials within relationships. In considering the motives, actions, circumstances, and power differentials in moral situations, we hope an ethics of responsibility facilitates the process of self-reflection. This process can expand from concern with our own actions and our own moral development to a broader consideration of the values of our profession.

> *Student affairs has been in a state of becoming for over a century and has become accepted as a traditional educational/service function of American higher education. . . .Whether the field formally "qualifies" as a profession at the present time or will qualify by the year 2000 should have little bearing on the quality of service provided and the quality of individual or collective performance and outcomes.* (Stamatakos, 1994, p. 547)

As we traverse the moral landscape in student affairs, we observe the products of this "process of becoming." Enhancing our knowledge of the terrain will expand our horizons and facilitate our progress on this journey.

REFERENCES

Baier, A. (1987). The need for more than justice. In M. Hanen & K. Nielsen (Eds.), *Science, Morality and Feminist Theory*. Calgary: University of Calgary Press.

Beauchamp, T., & Childress, J. F. (1994). *Principles of biomedical ethics*. (4th ed.). NY: Oxford University Press.

Carse, A. L. (1991). The 'voice of care': Implications for bioethical education. *The Journal of Medicine and Philosophy, 16*, 5-28.

Friedman, M. (1989). Feminism and modern friendship: Dislocating the community. *Ethics, 99*, 275-290.

Gilligan, C. (1982). *In a different voice: Psychological theory and women's development*. Cambridge, MA: Harvard University Press.

Gilligan, C. (1987). Moral orientation and moral development. In E. Kittay & D. T. Meyers (Eds.), *Women and moral theory* (pp. 19-33). Totawa, NJ: Rowman and Littlefield.

Held, V. (1987). Feminism and moral theory. In E. Kittay & D. Meyers (Eds.), *Women and moral theory*. Totowa, NJ: Rowman and Littlefield.

Held, V. (1993). *Feminist morality*. Chicago: University of Chicago Press.

Kuh, G. D. (1996). Guiding principles for creating learning environments for undergraduates. *Journal of College Student Development, 37*, 135-148.

Lebacqz, K. (1995). Feminism. In W. T. Reich (Ed.), *Encyclopedia of bioethics* (Rev. ed., pp. 808-818). NY: Macmillan.

Manning, R. (1992). *Speaking from the heart*. Lanham, MD: Rowman and Littlefield.

Niebuhr, H. R. (1963). *The responsible self: An essay in Christian moral philosophy*. NY: Harper Collins.

Noddings, N. (1984). *Caring: A feminine approach to ethics and moral education*. Berkeley, CA: University of California Press.

Ruddick, S. (1989). *Maternal thinking*. Boston: Beacon Press.

Stamatakos, L.C. (1994). Student affairs progress toward professionalism: Recommendations for action, part 2. In Rentz, A.L. (Ed.), *Student affairs: A profession's heritage* (pp. 536-550). Lanham, Maryland: University Press of America.

Tronto, J. (1993). *Moral boundaries*. NY: Routledge.

Walker, M. U. (1997). Picking up pieces: Lives, stories, and integrity. In D. T. Meyers (Ed.). *Feminists rethink the self* (pp. 62-84). Boulder, CO: Westview Press.

Walker, M. U. (1998). *Moral understandings: A feminist study in ethics*. NY: Routledge.

APPENDIX A

Suggested Readings in Ethics & Morality

GENERAL ETHICS

Aristotle. (1953). *The ethics of Aristotle: The Nichomachean ethics* (J.A.K. Thompson, Trans.). Middlesex, England: Penguin.

Baron, M. W., Pettit, P., & Slote, M. (1997). *Three methods of ethics.* Oxford: Blackwell.

Cahn, S. M., & Markie, P. (Eds.). (1998). *Ethics: History, theory, and contemporary issues.* NY: Oxford University Press.

Cooper, D.E. (Ed.). (1998). *Ethics: The classic readings.* Oxford: Blackwell.

Elliott, C. (1992). Where ethics comes from and what to do about it?. *Hastings Center Report, 22*(4), 28-35.

Fishkin, J.S. (1982). *The limits of obligation.* New Haven: Yale University Press.

Flew, A. (Ed.). (1979). *A dictionary of philosophy* (2nd edition). NY: St. Martin's.

Frankena, W. (1973). *Ethics* (2nd ed.). Englewood Cliffs, NJ: Prentice Hall.

Frankena, W. (1980) *Thinking about morality.* Ann Arbor, MI: The University of Michigan Press.

Komesaroff, P. A. (Ed.). (1995). *Troubled bodies: Critical perspectives on postmodernism medical ethics, and the body.* Durham, NC: Duke University Press.

MacIntyre, A. (1966). *A short history of ethics.* NY: Macmillan.

May, W. F. (1983). *The physician's covenant: Images of the healer in medical ethics.* Philadelphia: Westminster Press.

Rawls, J. (1971). *A theory of justice.* Cambridge, MA: Harvard University Press.

Rosen, B., & Caplan, A. L. (1980). *Ethics in the undergraduate curriculum.* Hastings-on-Hudson, NY: The Hastings Center.

Solomon, W. D. (1995). Ethics: Normative ethical theories. In W. T. Reich (Ed.) *Encyclopedia of bioethics* (Rev. ed., Vol 2, pp. 736-748). NY: Macmillan.

Warnock, M. (Ed.). (1962). *J. S. Mill's Utilitarianism, On Liberty, Essay on Bentham.* Middlesex, England: Penguin Books.

Wicks, A. C., Spielman, B. J., & Fletcher, J. C. (1995). Survey of ethical orientations and theories. In J. C. Fletcher, C. A. Hite, P. A. Lombardo, & M. F. Marshall (Eds.), *Introduction to clinical ethics* (pp. 239-247). Frederick, MD: University Publishing Group.

STUDENT AFFAIRS, HIGHER EDUCATION, AND ETHICS

American College Personnel Association [ACPA]. (1994). *The student learning imperative: Implications for student affairs*. Washington, DC: Author.

Baca, M. C., & Stein, R. H. (Eds.). (1983). *Ethical principles, practices, and problems in higher education*. Springfield, IL: Charles C. Thomas.

Barr, M. J., & Upcraft, M. L. (1990) Identifying challenges for the future in current practice. In M. J. Barr, M. L. Upcraft, & Associates (Eds.), *New futures for student affairs*. San Francisco: Jossey- Bass.

Barr, M. J., & Associates (Eds.). (1993). *Handbook of student affairs administration*. San Francisco, CA: Jossey-Bass.

Bloland, P. A., Stamatakos, L. C., & Rogers, R. R. (1994). *Reform in student affairs: A critique of student development*. Greensboro, NC: ERIC Counseling and Student Services Clearinghouse.

Cahn, S. M. (Ed.). (1990). *Morality, responsibility, and the university: Studies in academic ethics*. Philadelphia: Temple University Press.

Callahan, D. & Bok, S. (Eds.). (1980). *Ethics teaching in higher education*. NY: Plenum Press.

Canon, H. J., & Brown, R. D. (Eds.) (1985). *Applied ethics in student services*. (New Directions for Student Services, No, 30). San Francisco: Jossey-Bass.

Chickering, A. W., & Reisser, L. (1993). *Education and identity* (2nd edition). San Francisco: Jossey-Bass.

Fried, J. (Ed.). (1997). *Ethics for today's campus: New perspective on education, student development, and institutional management*. (New Directions for Student Services, No. 77). San Francisco: Jossey-Bass.

Gibbs, A. (1992). *Reconciling rights and responsibilities of colleges and students*. (ASHE-ERIC Higher Education Report No. 5). Washington, DC: Association for the Study of Higher Education.

Hoekema, D. A. (1994). *Campus rules and moral community: In place of* in loco parentis. Lanham, MD: Rowman & Littlefield.

Institute of Society, Ethics, and the Life Sciences. (1980). *The teaching of ethics in higher education*. Hastings-on-Hudson, NY: The Hastings Center.

Kaplin, W. A., & Lee, B. A. (1997). *A legal guide for student affairs professionals* (3rd Ed.). San Francisco: Jossey-Bass.

Kierstead, F. D., & Wagner, Jr., P. A. (1993). *The ethical, legal, and multicultural foundations of teaching*. Madison, WI: Brown & Benchmark.

Kitchener, K. S. (1984). Intuition, critical evaluation and ethical principles: The foundation for ethical decisions in counseling psychology. *Counseling Psychologist, 12*(3), 43-55.

Kitchener, K. S. (1985). Ethical principles and ethical decision in student affairs. In H. J. Canon and R. D. Brown (Eds.) *Ethical principles and ethical decision making in student affairs* (New Directions for Student Services, No. 30. pp.17-29). San Francisco: Jossey-Bass.

Kuh, G. D. (1996). Guiding principles for creating learning environments for undergraduates. *Journal of College Student Development, 37,* 135-148.

May, W. W. (Ed.). (1990). *Ethics and higher education.* NY: ACE/Macmillan.

McBee, M. L. (1994). Moral development: From direction to dialogue. In Rentz, A. L. (Ed.), *Student affairs: A profession's heritage* (pp. 567-574). Lanham, Maryland: University Press of America.

Mitchell, C. T. (Ed.). (1989). *Values in teaching and professional ethics.* Macon, GA: Mercer University Press.

Nash, R. J. (1997). Teaching philosophy of education as moral conversation: A lengthy memo to my graduate students. Fostering moral conversations in the college classroom. *Journal on Excellence in College Teaching, 7*(1).

Nash, R. J. (1996). *"Real world" ethics: Frameworks for educators and human service professionals.* NY: Teacher's College Press.

Nash, R. J. (1997). Teaching ethics in the student affairs classroom. *NASPA Journal, 35,* 3-19.

Nash, R. J. (1997). *Answering the "virtuecrats": A moral conversation on character education.* NY: Teacher's College Press.

Pascarella, E. T., & Terenzini, P. T. (1981). *How college affects students.* San Francisco: Jossey-Bass.

Payne, S. L., & Charnov, B. H. (Eds.). (1987). *Ethical dilemmas for academic professionals.* Springfield, IL: Charles C. Thomas..

Rich, J. M. (1984). *Professional ethics in education.* Springfield, IL: Charles C. Thomas.

Robinson, G. M. & Moulton, J. (1985). *Ethical problems in higher education.* Englewood Cliffs, NJ: Prentice-Hall.

Sola, P. A. (Ed.). (1984). *Ethics, education and administrative decisions: A book of readings.* NY: Peter Lang.

Stamatakos, L. C. (1994). Student affairs progress toward professionalism:

Recommendations for action. part 2. In Rentz, A.L. (Ed.), *Student affairs: A profession's heritage* (pp. 536-550). Lanham, Maryland: University Press of America, Inc.

Terenzini, P. T., Pascarella, E. T., & Blimling, G. S. (1996). Student's out-of-class experiences and their influences on learning and cognitive development: A literature review. *Journal of College Student Development, 37,* 149-162.

Upcraft, M. L., & Poole, T. G. (1991). Ethical issues and administrative policies. In P. L. Moore (Ed.) *Managing the political dimension of student affairs* (pp. 81-93). San Francisco: Jossey-Bass.

Whicker, M. L., & Kronenfeld, J. J. (1994). *Dealing with ethical dilemmas on campus.* Thousand Oaks, CA: Sage.

PRINCIPLES-BASED APPROACHES TO ETHICS

Beauchamp, T. L. (1996). The role of principles in practical ethics. In L. W. Sumner and J. Boyle (Eds.), *Philosophical perspectives on bioethics* (pp. 79-95). Toronto: University of Toronto Press.

Beauchamp, T. L., & Childress, J. F. (1994). *Principles of biomedical ethics* (4th ed.). NY: Oxford University Press.

Childress, J. F. (1994). Principles-oriented bioethics: An analysis and assessment from within. In E. R. DuBose, R. Hamel, & L. J. O'Connell (Eds.), *A matter of principles: Ferment in U.S. bioethics* (pp. 72-98). Valley Forge, PA: Trinity Press International.

Childress, J. F. (1997). The normative principles of medical ethics. In R. M. Veatch (Ed.)., *Medical Ethics* (2nd Ed., pp. 29-55). Sudbury, MA: Jones and Bartlett.

Clouser, K. D., & Gert, B. (1990). A critique of principlism. *The Journal of Medicine and Philosophy, 15*, 219-236.

DeGrazia, D. (1992). Moving forward in bioethical theory: Theories, cases, and specified principlism. *The Journal of Medicine and Philosophy, 17,* 511-539.

Hare, R. M. (1972). Principles. *Proceedings of the Aristotelian society, 73*, 1-18.

Englehardt, Jr., H. T. (1986). *The foundations of bioethics*. NY: Oxford University Press.

Gert, B., Culver, C. M., & Clouser, K. D. (1997). *Bioethics: A return to fundamentals.* NY: Oxford University Press.

Kant, I. (1981). *Groundings for the metaphysics of morals* (J. W. Ellington, Trans.). Indianapolis, IN: Hackett. (Original Work published in 1785)

Richardson, H. S. (1990). Specifying norms as a way to resolve concrete ethical problems. *Philosophy and Public Affairs 19*, 279-310.

Tunick, M. (1998). *Practices and principles: Approaches to ethical and legal judgment.* Princeton, NJ: Princeton University Press.

Veatch, R. M. (1981). *A theory of medical ethics.* NY: Basic Books.

Wallace, J. D. (1996). *Ethical norms, particular cases.* Ithaca, NY: Cornell University Press.

CASE-BASED APPROACHES TO ETHICS

Arras, J. D. (1991). Getting down to cases: The revival of casuistry in bioethics. *The Journal of Medicine and Philosophy, 16*(1), 29-51.

Arras, J. D. (1994). Principles and particularity: The roles of cases in bioethics. *Indiana Law Journal, 69*, 983-1014.

Carson, R. A. (1986). Case method. *Journal of Medical Ethics, 12*(1), 36-38.

Chambers, T. S. (1994). The bioethicist as author: The medical ethics case as rhetorical device. *Literature and Medicine, 13*(1), 60-78.

Fletcher, J. (1966). *Situation ethics*. Philadelphia: Westminster Press.

Fletcher, J. C., Hite, C. A., Lombardo, P. A., & Marshall, M. F. (Eds.). (1995). *Introduction to clinical ethics*. Frederick, MD: University Publishing Group.

Jonsen, A. R. (1986). Casuistry and clinical ethics. *Theoretical Medicine, 7*, 65-74.

Jonsen, A. R. (1991). Of balloons and bicycles or the relationship between ethical theory and practical judgment. *The Hastings Center Report, 21*(5), 14-16.

Jonsen, A. R (1991). Casuistry as methodology in clinical ethics. *Theoretical Medicine, 12*, 295-307.

Jonsen, A. R. (1995). Casuistry. In W. T. Reich (Ed.), *Encyclopedia of bioethics* (Rev. ed., Vol. 1, pp. 344-350). NY: Macmillan.

Jonsen, A. R., & Toulmin, S. (1988). *The abuse of casuistry*. Berkeley: University of California Press.

Juengst, E. T. (1989). Casuistry and the locus of certainty in ethics. *Medical Humanities Review, 3*(1), 19-27.

Kuczewski, M. G. (1997). *Fragmentation and consensus: Communitarian and casuist bioethics*. Washington, DC: Georgetown University Press.

Miller, R. B. (1994). Narrative and casuistry: A response to John Arras. *Indiana Law Journal, 69*, 1015-1019.

Miller, R. B. (1996). *Casuistry and modern ethics: A poetics of practical reasoning*. Chicago: University of Chicago Press.

Pascal, B. (1875). *The provincial letters*. (T. M'Crie, Trans.). London: Chatto and Windus. (Original work published 1656).

Toulmin, S. (1981). The tyranny of principles. *The Hastings Center Report, 11*(6), 31-39.

Wildes, K. W. (1993). The priesthood of bioethics and the return of casuistry. *The Journal of Medicine and Philosophy, 18*(1), 33-49.

Williams, S. H. (1994). Bioethics and epistemology: A response to Professor Arras. *Indiana Law Journal, 69*, 1021-1026.

VIRTUES-BASED APPROACHES TO ETHICS

Crisp, R., & Slote, M. (Eds.). (1997). *Virtue ethics.* NY: Oxford University Press.

Darling-Smith, B. (1993). *Can virtue be taught?* Notre Dame, IN: University of Notre Dame Press.

Drane, J. F. (1994). Character and the moral life: A virtue approach to biomedical ethics. In E. R. DuBose, R. Hamel, & L. J. O'Connell (Eds.), *A Matter of Principles: Ferment in U.S. Bioethics* (pp. 72-98). Valley Forge, PA: Trinity Press International.

Foot, P. (1978). *Virtues and vices and other essays in moral philosophy.* Berkeley: University of California Press.

Hauerwas, S. (1981). *A community of character.* Notre Dame, IN: University of Notre Dame Press.

Hauerwas, S. (1995). Virtue and character. In Warren T. Reich (ed.), *Encyclopedia of bioethics* (Rev. ed., pp. 2525-2532). NY: Macmillan.

Louden, R. B. (1984). On some vices of virtue ethics. *American Philosophical Quarterly 21*, 227-236.

MacIntyre, A. (1984). *After virtue: A study in moral theory.* Notre Dame, IN: University of Notre Dame Press.

Pence, G. E. (1984). Recent work on virtues. *American Philosophical Quarterly 21*, 281-297.

Pincoffs, E. (1971). Quandary ethics. *Mind, 80*, 552-571.

Pincoffs, E. L. (1986). *Quandaries and virtues: Against reductivism in ethics.* Lawrence, KS: University Press of Kansas.

Statman, D. (1997). *Virtue ethics: A critical reader.* Washington, DC: Georgetown University Press.

FEMINIST APPROACHES TO ETHICS

Baier, A. (1987). The need for more than justice. In M. Hanen & K. Nielsen (Eds.), *Science, Morality and Feminist Theory.* Calgary: University of Calgary Press.

Carse, A. L. (1991, February). The 'voice of care': Implications for bioethical education. *The Journal of Medicine and Philosophy, 16*(1), 5-28.

Friedman, M. (1989). Feminism and modern friendship: Dislocating the community. *Ethics, 99*, 275-290.

Gilligan, C. (1981). Moral development. In A. W. Chickering, & Associates (Eds.), *The modern American college* (pp. 139-157). San Francisco: Jossey-Bass.

Gilligan, C. (1993). *In a different voice: Psychological theory and women's development.* Cambridge, MA: Harvard University Press.

Gudorf, C. E. (1994). A feminist critique of biomedical principlism. In E. R. DuBose, R. Hamel, & L. J. O'Connell (Eds.), *A matter of principles: ferment in U.S. bioethics* (pp. 164-81). Valley Forge, PA: Trinity Press International.

Held, V. (1987). Feminism and moral theory. In E. Kittay & D. Meyers (Eds.), *Women and moral theory*. Totowa, NJ: Rowman and Littlefield.

Held, V. (1993). *Feminist morality*. Chicago: University of Chicago Press.

Jecker, N. S., & Reich, W. T. (1995). Contemporary ethic of care. In W. T. Reich (Ed.), *Encyclopedia of bioethics* (Rev. ed., pp. 336-344). NY: Macmillan.

Lebacqz, K. (1995). Feminism. In W. T. Reich (ed.), *Encyclopedia of bioethics* (Rev. ed., pp. 808-818). NY: Macmillan.

Manning, R. (1992). *Speaking from the heart*. Lanham, MD: Rowman and Littlefield.

Noddings, N. (1984). *Caring: A feminine approach to ethics and moral education*. Berkeley, CA: University of California Press.

Ruddick, S. (1989). *Material Thinking*. Boston: Beacon Press.

Tong, R. (1996). Feminist approaches to bioethics. In S. M. Wolf (Ed.), *Feminism and bioethics: Beyond reproduction* (pp. 67-94). NY: Oxford University Press.

Tronto, J. (1993). *Moral boundaries*. NY: Routledge.

Walker, M.U. (1997). Picking up pieces: Lives, stories, and integrity. In D.T. Meyers (Ed.). *Feminists rethink the self* (pp. 62-84). Boulder, CO: Westview Press.

Walker, M.U. (1998). *Moral understandings: A feminist study in ethics*. NY: Routledge.

APPENDIX B

Guidelines for Ethical Analysis of Cases

We include the following reference materials to guide you through analysis of difficult case situations. Chapters Three and Four offer a more complete description of how to use the first two methods. Please refer to the original articles or texts for further explication of these processes.

A PRINCIPLES-BASED PERSPECTIVE (BEAUCHAMP & CHILDRESS, 1994)

1. Describe the facts of the case, including *who*, *what*, *where*, *when*, and *why* considerations.
2. Describe what moral or professional principles are at stake.
3. Specify the principles to meet the circumstances of the case.
4. If more than one principle applies, how do they relate to each other? (complement, contradict, etc.)
5. Balance the principles and try to reach a compromise, or
6. Override one principle, keeping the following considerations in mind:
   a. The objective of breaking the rule should have a realistic prospect of achievement.
   b. No morally preferable alternative should be available.
   c. The main principle should be stronger in this case.
   d. The form of the infringement should be the least possible.
   e. The agent should seek to minimize the effects of the infringement.
7. Choose one course of action based on the previous considerations.
8. Evaluate your decision.

A CASE-BASED PERSPECTIVE (JONSEN, 1991 & FLETCHER, 1995)

1. Identify the particular features of the case, including the *who, what, where, when,* and *why* considerations (casuistry).
   a. Identify the topics in the case and rank them (ex. relationship with supervisor).
2. Identify the ethical considerations in the case (casuistry).
   a. What paradigm cases can guide you?
   b. Where does this case fit into the spectrum of cases?
   c. What professional or moral guidelines can assist your analysis of this case?
3. Decision making and implementation.
   a. What are the ethically justifiable options?
   b. How can you accomplish a satisfactory resolution of the case?
   c. Is legal consultation necessary?
4. Review and evaluate your decision.
   a. Is it justified by the circumstances and guidelines involved?
   b. Do you feel that it is consistent with your character?

ROBERT J. NASH'S CASE-BASED PERSPECTIVE (NASH 1997)

1. What are the major moral themes in the case?
2. What are the conflicts in the case that make it an ethical dilemma?
3. Who are the major stakeholders in the case?
4. What are some foreseeable consequences of the possible choices in the case? What are some foreseeable principles?
5. What are some viable alternatives to the possible courses of action in the case?
6. What are some important background beliefs you ought to consider in the case?
7. What are some of your initial intuitions and feelings regarding the case?

8. What choices would you make if you were to act in character in the case?
9. What does your profession's code of ethics say regarding key moral principles in the case?
10. What is your decision in the case?

REFERENCES

Beauchamp, T. L., & Childress, J. F. (1994). *Principles of biomedical ethics* (4th ed.). NY: Oxford University Press.

Jonsen, A. R (1991). Casuistry as methodology in clinical ethics. *Theoretical Medicine, 12*, 295-307.

Nash, R. J. (1997). *Answering the "virtuecrats": A moral conversation on character education.* NY: Teacher's College Press.

Wicks, A. C., Spielman, B. J., & Fletcher, J. C. (1995). Survey of ethical orientations and theories. In J. C. Fletcher, C. A. Hite, P.A. Lombardo, & M. F. Marshall (Eds.), *Introduction to clinical ethics* (pp. 239-247). Frederick, MD: University Publishing Group.

APPENDIX C

National Association of Student Personnel Administrators

STANDARDS OF PROFESSIONAL PRACTICE

The National Association of Student Personnel Administrators [NASPA] is an organization of colleges, universities, agencies, and professional educators whose members are committed to providing services and education that enhance student growth and development. The association seeks to promote student personnel work as a profession which requires personal integrity, belief in the dignity and worth of individuals, respect for individual differences and diversity, a commitment to service, and dedication to the development of individuals and the college community through education. NASPA supports student personnel work by providing opportunities for its members to expand knowledge and skills through professional education and experience. The following standards were endorsed by NASPA at the December 1990 board of directors meeting in Washington, D.C.

1. **Professional Services**

    Members of NASPA fulfill the responsibilities of their position by supporting the educational interests, rights, and welfare of students in accordance with the mission of the employing institution.

2. **Agreement with Institutional Mission and Goals**

    Members who accept employment with an educational institution subscribe to the general mission and goals of the institution.

3. **Management of Institutional Resources**

    Members seek to advance the welfare of the employing institution through accountability for the proper use of institutional funds, personnel, equipment, and other resources. Members inform appropriate officials of conditions which may be potentially disruptive or damaging to the institution's mission, personnel, and property.

4. **Employment Relationship**

    Members honor employment relationships. Members do not commence new duties or obligations at another institution under a new contractual agreement until termination of an existing contract, unless otherwise agreed to by the member and the member's current and new supervisors. Members adhere to professional practices in securing positions and employment relationships.

5. **Conflict of Interest**

    Members recognize their obligation to the employing institution and seek to avoid private interests, obligations, and transactions which are in conflict of interest or give the appearance of impropriety. Members clearly distinguish between statements and actions which represent their own personal views and those which represent their employing institution when important to do so.

6. **Legal Authority**

    Members respect and acknowledge all lawful authority. Members refrain from conduct involving dishonesty, fraud, deceit, and misrepresentation or unlawful discrimination. NASPA recognizes that legal issues are often ambiguous, and members should seek the advice of counsel as appropriate. Members demonstrate concern for the legal, social codes and moral expectations of the communities in which they live and work even when the dictates of one's conscience may require behavior as a private citizen which is not in keeping with these codes/expectations.

7. **Equal Consideration and Treatment of Others**

    Members execute professional responsibilities with fairness and impartiality and show equal consideration to individuals regardless of status or position. Members respect individuality and promote an appreciation of human diversity in higher education. In keeping with the mission of their respective institution and remaining cognizant of federal, state, and local laws, they do not discriminate on the basis of race, religion, creed, gender, age, national origin, sexual orientation, or physical disability. Members do not engage in or tolerate harassment in any form and should exercise professional judgment in entering into intimate relationships with those for whom they have any supervisory, evaluative, or instructional responsibility.

8. **Student Behavior**

    Members demonstrate and promote responsible behavior and support actions that enhance personal growth and development of students. Members foster conditions designed to ensure a student's acceptance of responsibility for his/her own behavior. Members inform and educate students as to sanctions or constraints on student behavior which may result from violations of law or institutional policies.

9. **Integrity of Information and Research**

    Members ensure that all information conveyed to others is accurate and in appropriate context. In their research and publications, members conduct and report research studies to assure accurate interpretation of findings, and they adhere to accepted professional standards of academic integrity.

10. **Confidentiality**

    Members ensure that confidentiality is maintained with respect to all privileged communications and to educational and professional records considered confidential. They inform all parties of the nature and/or limits of confidentiality. Members share information only in accordance with institutional policies and relevant statutes when given the informed consent or when required to prevent personal harm to themselves or others.

11. **Research Involving Human Subjects**

    Members are aware of and take responsibility for all pertinent ethical principles and institutional requirements when planning any research activity dealing with human subjects. (See Ethical Principles in the

Conduct of Research with Human Participants, Washington, D.C.: American Psychological Association, 1982.)

12. **Representation of Professional Competence**

    Members at all times represent accurately their professional credentials, competencies, and limitations and act to correct any misrepresentations of these qualifications by others. Members make proper referrals to appropriate professionals when the member's professional competence does not meet the task or issue in question.

13. **Selection and Promotion Practices**

    Members support nondiscriminatory, fair employment practices by appropriately publicizing staff vacancies, selection criteria, deadlines, and promotion criteria in accordance with the spirit and intent of equal opportunity policies and established legal guidelines and institutional policies.

14. **References**

    Members, when serving as a reference, provide accurate and complete information about candidates, including both relevant strengths and limitations of a professional and personal nature.

15. **Job Definitions and Performance Evaluation**

    Members clearly define with subordinates and supervisors job responsibilities and decision-making procedures, mutual expectations, accountability procedures, and evaluation criteria.

16. **Campus Community**

    Members promote a sense of community among all areas of the campus by working cooperatively with students, faculty, staff, and others outside the institution to address the common goals of student learning and development. Members foster a climate of collegiality and mutual respect in their work relationships.

17. **Professional Development**

    Members have an obligation to continue personal professional growth and to contribute to the development of the profession by enhancing personal knowledge and skills, sharing ideas and information, improving professional practices, conducting and reporting research, and participating in association activities. Members promote and facilitate the professional growth of staff and they emphasize ethical standards in professional preparation and development programs.

18. **Assessment**

    Members regularly and systematically assess organizational structures, programs, and services to determine whether the developmental goals and needs of students are being met and to assure conformity to published standards and guidelines such as those of the Council for the Advancement of Standards for Student Services/Development Programs [CAS]. Members collect data which include responses from students and other significant constituencies and make assessment results available to appropriate institutional officials for the purpose of revising and improving program goals and implementation.

APPENDIX D

American College Personnel Association

STATEMENT OF ETHICAL PRINCIPLES AND STANDARDS
AS PRESENTED BY THE ACPA STANDING COMMITTEE
ON ETHICS AND APPROVED BY THE ACPA
EXECUTIVE COUNCIL, NOVEMBER 1992

PREAMBLE

The American College Personnel Association [ACPA] is an association whose members are dedicated to enhancing the worth, dignity, potential, and uniqueness of each individual within post-secondary educational institutions and thus to the service of society. ACPA members are committed to contributing to the comprehensive education of the student, protecting human rights, advancing knowledge of student growth and development, and promoting the effectiveness of institutional programs, services, and organizational units. As a means of supporting these commitments, members of ACPA subscribe to the following principles and standards of ethical conduct. Acceptance of membership in ACPA signifies that the member agrees to adhere to the provisions of this statement.

This statement is designed to address issues particularly relevant to college student affairs practice. Persons charged with duties in various functional areas of higher education are also encouraged to consult ethical standards specific to their professional responsibilities.

USE OF THIS STATEMENT

The principal purpose of this statement is to assist student affairs professionals in regulating their own behavior by sensitizing them to potential ethical problems and by providing standards useful in daily practice. Observance of ethical behavior also benefits fellow professionals and students due to the effect of modeling. Self-regulation is the most effective and preferred means of assuring ethical behavior. If, however, a professional observes conduct by a fellow professional that seems contrary to the provisions of this document, several courses of action are available.

- Initiate a private conference. Because unethical conduct often is due to a lack of awareness or understanding ethical standards, a private conference with the professional(s) about the conduct in question is an important initial line of action. This conference, if pursued in a spirit of collegiality and sincerity, often may resolve the ethical concern and promote future ethical conduct.

- Pursue institutional remedies. If Private consultation does not produce the desired results, institutional channels for resolving alleged ethical improprieties may be pursued. All student affairs divisions should have a widely-publicized process for addressing allegations of ethical misconduct.

- Contact ACPA Ethics Committee. If the ACPA member is unsure about whether a particular activity or practice falls under the provisions of this statement, the Ethics Committee may be contacted in writing. The member should describe in reasonable detail (omitting data that would identify the person(s) as much as possible) the potentially unethical conduct or practices and the circumstances surrounding the situation. Members of the Committee or others in the Association will provide the member with a summary of opinions regarding the ethical appropriateness of the conduct or practice in question. Because these opinions are based on limited information, no specific situation or action will be judged unethical. The responses rendered by the Committee are advisory only and are not an official statement on behalf of ACPA.

- Request consultation from ACPA Ethics Committee. If the institution wants further assistance in resolving the controversy, an institutional representative may request on-campus consultation. Provided all parties to the controversy agree, a team of consultants selected by the Ethics Committee will visit the campus at the institution's expense to hear the allegations and to review the facts and circumstances. The team will advise institutional leadership on possible actions consistent with both the content and spirit of the ACPA Statement of Ethical Principles and Standards. Compliance with the recommendations is voluntary. No sanctions will be imposed by ACPA. Institutional leaders remain responsible for assuring ethical conduct and practice. The consultation team will maintain confidentiality surrounding the process to the extent possible.
- Submit complaint to ACPA Ethics Committee. If the alleged misconduct may be a violation of the ACPA Statement of Ethical Principles and Standards, the person charged is unavailable or produces unsatisfactory results, then proceedings against the individual(s) may be brought to the ACPA Ethics Committee for review. Details regarding the procedures may be obtained by contacting the Executive Director at ACPA Headquarters.

ETHICAL PRINCIPLES

No statement of ethical standards can anticipate all situations that have ethical implications. When student affairs professionals are presented with dilemmas that are not explicitly addressed herein, five ethical principles may be used in conjunction with the four enumerated standards (Professional Responsibility and Competence. Student Learning and Development. Responsibility to the Institution. Responsibility to Society) to assist in making decisions and determining appropriate courses of action.

Ethical principles should guide the behaviors of professionals in everyday practice. Principles, however, are not just guidelines for reaction when something goes wrong or when a complaint is raised. Adhering to ethical principles also calls for action. These principles include the following:

- Act to benefit others. Service to humanity is the basic tenet underlying student affairs practice. Hence, student affairs professionals exist to: [a] promote healthy social, physical, academic, moral, cognitive, career, and personality development of students; [b] bring a developmental perspective to the institution's total educational process and learning environment; [c] contribute to the effective functioning of the institution; and [d] provide programs and services consistent with this principle.
- Promote justice. Student affairs professionals are committed to assuring fundamental fairness for all individuals within the academic community. In pursuit of this goal, the principles of impartiality, equity, and reciprocity (treating others as one would desire to be treated) are basic. When there are greater needs than resources available or when the interests of constituencies conflict, justice requires honest consideration of all claims and requests and equitable (not necessarily equal) distribution of goods and services. A crucial aspect of promoting justice is demonstrating an appreciation for human differences and opposing intolerance and bigotry concerning these differences. Important human differences include, but are not limited to, characteristics such as age, culture, ethnicity, gender, disabling condition, race, religion, or sexual/affectional orientation.
- Respect autonomy. Student affairs professionals respect and promote individual autonomy and privacy. Students' freedom of choice and action are not restricted unless their actions significantly interfere with the welfare of others or the accomplishment of the institution's mission.
- Be faithful. Student affairs professionals are truthful, honor agreements, and are trustworthy in the performance of their duties.
- Do no harm. Student affairs professionals do not engage in activities that

cause either physical or psychological damage to others. In addition to their personal actions, student affairs professionals are especially vigilant to assure that the institutional policies do not: [a] hinder students' opportunities to benefit from the learning experiences available in the environment; [b] threaten individuals' self-worth, dignity, or safety; or [c] discriminate unjustly or illegally.

ETHICAL STANDARDS

Four ethical standards related to primary constituencies with whom student affairs professionals work—fellow professionals, students, educational institutions, and society—are specified.

1.0   Professional Responsibility and Competence. Student affairs professionals are responsible for promoting students' learning and development, enhancing the understanding of student life, and advancing the profession and its ideals. They possess the knowledge, skills, emotional stability, and maturity to discharge responsibilities as administrators, advisors, consultants, counselors, programmers, researchers, and teachers. High levels of professional competence are expected in the performance of their duties and responsibilities. They ultimately are responsible for the consequences of their actions or inaction.

As ACPA members, student affairs professionals will:

1.1   Adopt a professional lifestyle characterized by use of sound theoretical principles and a personal value system congruent with the basic tenets of the profession.

1.2   Contribute to the development of the profession (e.g. recruiting students to the profession, serving professional organizations, educating new professionals, improving professional practices, and conducting and reporting research).

1.3 Maintain and enhance professional effectiveness by improving skills and acquiring new knowledge.

1.4 Monitor their personal and professional functioning and effectiveness and seek assistance from appropriate professionals as needed.

1.5 Represent their professional credentials, competencies, and limitations accurately and correct any misrepresentations of these qualifications by others.

1.6 Establish fees for professional services after consideration of the ability of the recipient to pay. They will provide some services, including professional development activities for colleagues, for little or no remuneration.

1.7 Refrain from attitudes or actions that impinge on colleagues' dignity, moral code, privacy, worth, professional functioning, and/or personal growth.

1.8 Abstain from sexual harassment.

1.9 Abstain from sexual intimacies with colleagues or with staff for whom they have supervisory, evaluative, or instructional responsibility.

1.10 Refrain from using their positions to seek unjustified personal gains, sexual favors, unfair advantages, or unearned goods and services not normally accorded those in such positions.

1.11 Inform students of the nature and/or limits of confidentiality. They will share information about the students only in accordance with institutional policies and applicable laws, when given their permission, or when required to prevent personal harm to themselves or others.

1.12 Use records and electronically stored information only to accomplish legitimate, institutional purposes and to benefit students.

1.13 Define job responsibilities, decision-making procedures, mutual expectations, accountability procedures, and evaluation criteria with subordinates and supervisors.

1.14 Acknowledge contributions by others to program development, program implementation, evaluations, and reports.

1.15 Assure that participation by staff in planned activities that emphasize self-disclosure or other relatively intimate or personal involvement is voluntary and that the leader(s) of such activities do not have administrative, supervisory, or evaluative authority over participants.

1.16 Adhere to professional practices in securing positions: [a] represent education and experiences accurately; [b] respond to offers promptly; [c] accept only those positions they intend to assume; [d] advise current employer and all institutions at which applications are pending immediately when they sign a contract; and [e] inform their employers at least thirty days before leaving a position.

1.17 Gain approval of research plans involving human subjects from the institutional committee with oversight responsibility prior to initiation of the study. In the absence of such a committee, they will seek to create procedures to protect the rights and assure the safety of research participants.

1.18 Conduct and report research studies accurately. They will not engage in fraudulent research nor will they distort or misrepresent their data or deliberately bias their results.

1.19 Cite previous works on a topic when writing or when speaking to professional audiences.

1.20 Acknowledge major contributions to research projects and professional writings through joint authorships with the principal contributor listed first. They will acknowledge minor technical or professional contributions in notes or introductory statements.

1.21 Not demand co-authorship of publications when their involvement was ancillary or unduly pressure others for joint authorship.

1.22 Share original research data with qualified others upon request.

1.23 Communicate the results of any research judged to be of value to other professionals and not withhold results reflecting unfavorably on specific institutions, programs, services, or prevailing opinion.

1.24 Submit manuscripts for consideration to only one journal at a time. They will not seek to publish previously published or accepted-for-publication materials in other media or publications without first informing all editors and/or publishers concerned. They will make appropriate references in the text and receive permission to use if copyrights are involved.

1.25 Support professional preparation program efforts by providing assistantships, practica, field placements, and consultation to students and faculty.

As ACPA members, preparation program faculty will:

1.26 Inform prospective graduate students of program expectations, predominant theoretical orientations, skills needed for successful completion, and employment of recent graduates.

1.27 Assure that required experiences involving self-disclosure are communicated to prospective graduate students. When the program offers experiences that emphasize self-disclosure or other relatively intimate or personal involvement (e.g., group or individual counseling or growth groups), professionals must not have current or anticipated administrative, supervisory, or evaluative authority over participants.

1.28 Provide graduate students with a broad knowledge base consisting of theory, research, and practice.

1.29 Inform graduate students of the ethical responsibilities and standards of the profession.

1.30 Assess all relevant competencies and interpersonal functioning of students throughout the program, communicate these assessments to students, and take appropriate corrective actions including dismissal when warranted.

1.31 Assure that field supervisors are qualified to provide supervision to graduate students and are informed of their ethical responsibilities in this role.

2.0 Student Learning and Development. Student development is an essential purpose of higher education, and the pursuit of this aim is a major responsibility of student affairs. Development is complex and includes cognitive, physical, moral, social, career, spiritual, personality, and educational dimensions. Professionals must be sensitive to the variety of backgrounds, cultures, and personal characteristics evident in the student population and use appropriate theoretical perspectives to identify learning opportunities and to reduce barriers that inhibit development.

As ACPA members, student affairs professionals will:

2.1 Treat students as individuals who possess dignity, worth, and the ability to be self-directed.

2.2 Avoid dual relationships with students (e.g., counselor/employer, supervisor/best friend, or faculty/sexual partner) that may involve incompatible roles and conflicting responsibilities.

2.3 Abstain from sexual harassment.

2.4 Abstain from sexual intimacies with clients or with students for whom they have supervisory, evaluative, or instructional responsibility.

2.5 Inform students of the conditions under which they may receive assistance and the limits of confidentiality when the counseling relationship is initiated.

2.6 Avoid entering or continuing helping relationships if benefits to students are unlikely. They will refer students to appropriate specialists and recognize that if the referral is declined, they are not obligated to continue the relationship.

2.7 Inform students about the purpose of assessment and make explicit the planned use of results prior to assessment.

2.8 Provide appropriate information to students prior to and following the use of any assessment procedure to place results in proper perspective with other relevant factors (e.g., socioeconomic, ethnic, cultural, and gender related experiences).

2.9   Confront students regarding issues, attitudes, and behaviors that have ethical implications.

3.0   Responsibility to the Institution. Institutions of higher education provide the context for student affairs practice. Institutional mission, policies, organizational structure, and culture, combined with individual judgment and professional standards, define and delimit the nature and extent of practice. Student affairs professionals share responsibility with other members of the academic community for fulfilling the institutional mission. Responsibility to promote the development of individual students and to support the institution's policies and interests require that professionals balance competing demands.

As ACPA members, student affairs professionals will:

3.1   Contribute to their institution by supporting its mission, goals, and policies.

3.2   Seek resolution when they and their institution encounter substantial disagreements concerning professional or personal values.
Resolution may require sustained efforts to modify institutional policies and practices or result in voluntary termination of employment.

3.3   Recognize that conflicts among students, colleagues, or the institution should be resolved without diminishing appropriate obligations to any party involved.

3.4   Assure that information provided about the institution is factual and accurate.

3.5   Inform appropriate officials of conditions that may be disruptive or damaging to their institution.

3.6 Inform supervisors of conditions or practices that may restrict institutional or professional effectiveness.

3.7 Recognize their fiduciary responsibility to the institution. They will assure that funds for which they have oversight are expended following established procedures and in ways that optimize value, are accounted for properly, and contribute to the accomplishment of the institution's mission. They also will assure equipment, facilities, personnel, and other resources are used to promote the welfare of the institution and students.

3.8 Restrict their private interests, obligations, and transactions in ways to minimize conflicts of interest or the appearance of conflicts of interest. They will identify their personal views and actions as private citizens from those expressed or undertaken as institutional representatives.

3.9 Collaborate and share professional expertise with members of the academic community.

3.10 Evaluate programs, services, and organizational structure regularly and systematically to assure conformity to published standards and guidelines. Evaluations should be conducted using rigorous evaluation methods and principles, and the results should be made available to appropriate institutional personnel.

3.11 Evaluate job performance of subordinates regularly and recommend appropriate actions to enhance professional development and improve performance.

3.12 Provide fair and honest assessments of colleagues' job performance.

3.13 Seek evaluations of their job performance and/or services they provide.

3.14 Provide training to student affairs search and screening committee members who are unfamiliar with the profession.

3.15 Disseminate information that accurately describes the responsibilities of position vacancies, required qualifications, and the institution.

3.16 Follow a published interview and selection process that periodically notifies applicants of their status.

4.0 Responsibility to Society. Student affairs professionals, both as citizens and practitioners, have a responsibility to contribute to the improvement of the communities in which they live and work. They respect individuality and recognize that worth is not diminished by characteristics such as age, culture, ethnicity, gender, disabling condition, race, religion, or sexual/affectional orientation. Student affairs professionals work to protect human rights and promote an appreciation of human diversity in higher education.

As ACPA members, student affairs professionals will:

4.1 Assist students in becoming productive and responsible citizens.

4.2 Demonstrate concern for the welfare of all students and work for constructive change on behalf of students.

4.3 Not discriminate on the basis of age, culture, ethnicity, gender, disabling condition, race, religion, or sexual/affectional orientation. They will work to modify discriminatory practices.

4.4 Demonstrate regard for social codes and moral expectations of the communities in which they live and work. They will recognize that violations of accepted moral and legal standards may involve their clients, students, or colleagues in damaging personal conflicts and may impugn the integrity of the profession, their own reputations, and that of the employing institution.

4.5 Report to the appropriate authority any condition that is likely to harm their clients and/or others.